Follow Next to Me:
Hope for Schizoaffective Disorder

SARA PAULSEN

DEDICATION

Dear Jordan,

I'll wait for you…If you wait for me
You're my missing half
The part that I need
The piece that fills
My carnal need
You are the one
That makes me be the best woman I can ever be

I'll wait for you if that is your wish
I'll do your bidding for just a kiss
I'll cross the sand and swim in the sea
I'll wait for you if you wait for me

I love you more than one woman should
I love you more than I thought I could
You are my finish my one my soul
Your heartfelt love it makes me whole

I love you

~ One ~

Push, push, push--that's Larry's game. What can he force me to do that I don't want to? You would be surprised at what I have done just to please him. I want to tear off my skin at the very thought of it. Why would I do it then? Because he doesn't stop. He lives between my ears screaming, playing his game for hours, days. Over and over. Do this, do it now. Right now. Who else could be trusted? Threats sing throughout my body sucking away my freewill. You are thinking that I should just not listen to it and he will go away. Screw you. How exactly would I do that? Cut my ears off? Even that has been proven not to be helpful. Really imagine what I am saying here is real because that is exactly what it is. Reality, my reality. You would do just about anything to make his voice stop. If you could silence the madness wouldn't you?

Of course.

But there is a problem. Once I give in Maggie is there waiting to make me feel guilty about whatever Larry made me do or even something I did one my own. Her words ring and vibrate in my ears. I am a coward, I ruin everything and everyone, and I don't deserve anything. Cut. Get a razor blade. Cut. It will make you feel better. No one should have to be around me. I deserve to live my life alone. I don't deserve to be alive. She takes away my will to live. Come on, give up, you are never going to do the right thing. I can hear my heartbeat. It's thumping, jumping, whacking against the walls and doorways and down the shitty staircase that she loves to throw me down. Here comes my stalker. Push and push and yell some more. She digs her dirty index finger into my chest. You're an asshole, you're a loser. You'll amount to nothing. I have heard it all too many times. Of course, she is always right. I am now a product of my own shimmering hallucinations. Killing my desires, my ambition, my relationships, and even worse, my free will.

You would think that this would be enough for me to push them away. But they are woven into my soul. They make me let go of who I am. The worse part is when they argue. Imagine two people, who you have grown to hate, fighting back and forth about everything you have done wrong all day long. All of my faults are ignited. And it gets louder and louder making a blaze that's impossible to ignore. Arriving unwelcomed. Walking around, pacing, ear to ear, wanting me to listen to them constantly. Threading my mind with hostile wire. Tying up my perspective with their words, barbed and frightened, dulled and tightened. Larry and Maggie are the tiny bits of that fence. Cutting me each time I try to jump over and run away. As I sprint down the street a panic floods over me and I can't, I can't move. I freeze in a cold sweat. I am consumed because they won't leave, and surprisingly, I can no longer live without the grating sound of their voices. I don't know who I am when they take a break. The occasional silence frightens me. I can't live life how it is supposed to be lived. There is duct tape all over my happiness.

My first memory is petting my imaginary friend, Follow, as she walked next to me through the blueberry field next to my house. Her cotton wool fur would curl up next to my leg when we were together. She was so graceful that you couldn't hear her land when she jumped off my lap. Just like most English Cocker Spaniels, she didn't like being alone. She had a happy disposition and was continuously wagging her tail. She was constantly pregnant since she was a hussy. Hussy was word that my grandmother used to describe the teenagers that would hang out at Old Orchard Beach whose baggy Maine t-shirts would hang over their short shorts. At the time, I didn't really know what that even meant, but I knew it made my family laugh so I kept saying it.

We would tell each other secrets and play Legos. I loved to draw my family and telephones. Red was my favorite color. I wanted to be just like Mary Lou Retton. My parents had started me in dance classes when I was very young because I was terribly uncoordinated. I got a pair of red-framed glasses with plastic strawberries on the corners and started dancing. I dressed in my electric blue unitard for tap and pink tights for ballet class every week. I lived for it. My stereo would blast the voices of Madonna, Whitney Houston, and Prince. But what I really enjoyed was my Thriller record. I played it over and over until even Follow knew the lyrics to "Billie Jean" and "Beat it". I would put my flashiest winter glove on my left hand and wiggle up in my room.

The whole second floor of the house was my room; all mine. It was originally the attic but they renovated it to give me more space and privacy. It seemed like I was never bored. I could always find some way to be entertained unlike some other children I knew who always needed someone to play with them. I liked to pretend to be Nancy Drew. I would sit out on the swing with a small spiral notebook and pencil. I spent the afternoons recording all the happenings. Scribbling down exactly which cars, license plates, and people were around. I would speculate as to what I thought they were up to. To have a good Nancy Drew day, I would be able to connect the day's events into some kind of conspiracy. There was always something new and entertaining to accomplish. I couldn't wait until my talent was recognized. All my practice tape recording sessions of "The Sara Show" would pay off. I just knew I would be a fantastic talk show host. I was very good at being alone, probably because I never felt alone. After all, Follow was always at my side. My mother wanted me to be a "social butterfly", but somehow I knew that that dream just was not going to happen.

Half a mile up the street were my father's parents. Born in 1919, my grandfather was a self employed cabinetmaker and woodworker. He built their house just before he was drafted when the buzz of Route 1 wasn't just a block away. If you see pictures of when it was first built, there isn't a single home or road in sight. Grandpa's parents dragged him and his brother over here from Denmark when he was eight for a better life. His father got four cents per hour cleaning chimneys to provide for the whole family. If only the American Dream was the way it is portrayed in movies. When they got here food was scarce and expensive. They didn't know the language and no one even knew where Demark was. Here in Maine if you speak a different language most people will assume that you are French Canadian. As a family, they would collect all the food they could from Sebago Lake. Then nail the eels to the birch trees in the sunlight until they became nice and crispy for dinner.

He was very determined to be secure and provide a good life for Grandma. A direct descendent from the Mayflower, Harriett Alice was about as American as you can get. Apparently, according to our genealogy I am a Daughter of the American Revolution. They got married young and were still in love after more than sixty years marriage. "Isn't she just beautiful?" he would say to me as he watched her cook. He called her "Hattie". He was "Vern" short for Vernon. They were at peace still flirting and looking at each other with love and passion. Having them as a role model made me believe that true lasting love is possible. Even after she passed away, he would spend half an hour each night laying on his side of the bed telling her about his day. They did not adopt me but they were as much my parents as my real parents were. I spent more quality time with them over the years. I could tell them anything. I could be anyone and they would still love me.

My parents were seventeen years apart. When my mother was ten she was living right next to my father for a few years. He used to call her Spider because apparently she was very hairy. Little did he know that he would spend the rest of his life trying to get out of her web. They lost touch and then met again later in life. I really don't know how. It was never explained to me. But when my mother was about twenty-five she married my father and moved into the house that he had built years ago with his father. Pretty soon I came along and within just a few months they were not getting along. My father stayed in a motel just half a mile away so he could still see me every day. Somehow they must have resolved their issues because he moved back after a month or so. My mother had her own construction company and was rapidly building developments in Cumberland County. My father stopped being in the Marines and moved into mechanical engineering. I never once had a babysitter. Neither one of my parents dared to leave me with someone else. Well, either that or they never really wanted to be alone. Did they have anything to say to each other anymore? I had become the only commonality in their relationship.

Before I started school, I would spend the days with Grandpa. Just down the street, my grandfather made a smart investment by purchasing huge building on Route 1. His woodshop was the entire basement. It had every woodworking tool and machine, large tables to work on, and lots of sawdust. I sat on his lap listening the high pitched creak of his chair while trying to learn everything there is to know about how to make cabinets, balusters', bookcases, the works. I began to mimic his steady whistle while I was concentrating.

Thanks to the United States Army, who had handed him two packs on arrival to boot camp, he loved his Camels. This addiction would eventually be the means to his end. I carried a pencil in my shirt pocket like he did. It was always sharpened and ready to write down one measurement or another. He always grabbed for his pencil after he quit smoking thinking his pack of cigarettes was still in his pocket and he might be able to get another drag. He was incredibly busy for being retired. Grandpa was some kind of small town celebrity. Scarborough locals (police officers, fellow schoolmates, the gay pastor from across the street) would visit him, in and out all day. He was a collector of the town's gossip. His police scanner was constantly humming with juicy information. It was after all the best way to be the first to know what's happening to those around you. He had one in every room of the house. He even had one attached to his belt at his hip at all times. It would drive people crazy when they would visit because he wouldn't turn down the volume. But somehow it became relaxing to me. I knew I was home.

~ Two~

When my uncle Nate graduated from a pastry school in Oklahoma, Grandpa set him up with his own diner on the first floor. "The Coffee Shop" we all called it. My grandfather paid all the bills and set him up with an apartment in the other half of the building for his wife and child. He had no bills, no boss, or work ethic. Hot dogs and donuts were his specialty. It was the place to be if you were looking for a fifty-cent cup of coffee with unlimited free refills and plenty of ashtrays. The hours were 7am to 2pm. Nate would later fake a back injury because this was all too much. I was never quite sure what he was looking for. But for a while there it was moderately successful, especially at lunchtime.

Grandpa had his own table by the windows. He would sit at the head waiting as friends tricked in to fill up the black vinyl seats. On the second floor were a series of apartments rented out to gay male couples that couldn't find housing. When people teased him about his clientele he wouldn't back down, "You couldn't find better tenants", he would say proudly. "Careful when you bend over around the faggots. They are always ready to jump you, just you see." Grandpa's face would get red and then he would mutter how ignorant they were. Also in the building was the West Scarborough Post Office, which doesn't exist anymore, where my grandmother worked part time.

When dad was in the Marines he gave his father some money and told him to buy any piece of land that seemed like a good deal. He found us thirty-six acres of land, very close to his house, which was mostly forest and old cow paths. When he returned, the two of them built my house. Originally, it was meant to be the perfect bachelor pad for my father but my mother crashed on that dream. Conveniently, one path led to The Coffee Shop. It was about a mile away.

I loved to escape into the woods and pretend I was running away from home. I would become Little Red Riding Hood or play Hansel and Gretel. Mom always tried the reverse psychology technique to keep me from fleeing. You know, she tried to encourage me to go so I wouldn't go. But what she didn't realize was that I didn't care what she thought or wanted. This was about me, not her. I would pack up my Cinderella suitcase with my day of the week underwear, leggings, and two headbands. I refused to wear jeans. They were far too uncomfortable. Two cans of Spagetti0's and a bottle of water were sufficient. Of course, I would always take Follow with me along with my favorite scratch and sniff My Little Pony whose butt smelt like strawberries. In two days time, I would come home with my teeth stained from the wild blueberries near the power lines.

Preschool was the first time I felt like the outside world noticed me. My language skills and ability to retain knowledge were stronger than other kids my age from having conversations with Follow. I memorized all the types of dinosaurs and sang songs. I got a sticker for every book I read. I brought Follow to Show and Tell, which lead to an emergency parent-teacher conference. It was time for the talk. I was too old to have an imaginary friend. "Why don't you have her have to put a penny in a jar every time she says Follow's name?" As if Follow was now to be considered a swear word in my own home. Did my teacher even go to school? Who was this idiot? I cried. No one could take Follow away from me.

When the school day was over all of us would all gather on the staircase and wait for our parents to pick us up. I remember one-day mom was late. It had only been a few days since I had been told to never speak of Follow again. Did she forget me? I should have told them Follow was gone. But that wasn't the problem. Mom had a small accident on a job site. It made me worried anyway. From now on, I would just tell everyone that Follow had disappeared. It will make them feel better, I thought. What had once been a source of stories and laughter now lead to shaking heads and nervous glances. When had I crossed the line? At what age did this become weird?

But Follow never really went away. She is with me in spirit. If I am lonely or sad or devastated or heartbroken, she is the friend I have never had any doubts about. But our relationship, like all others, shifts. When life feels balanced Follow takes a back seat but remains there just in case of a rainy day.

In the red room, we had this humongous computer. It was one of the first IBM personal computers. Instead of having the hard drive inside the computer, I remember there were a series of four or so black, heavy hard drives that were each about the size of a large textbook that you slid in the bottom. Depending on what you wanted to do you would put in a different drive. I didn't know any other kids that had one and even in my first several years of school we had to use typewriters. I would use it to write small paragraphs about my day, print them out, and glue them in my diary. Mostly, I wrote about the weather or an upcoming holiday. I learned to type before any other kids my age. I also learned the wonders of old school Tetris.

When I started kindergarten, it became even more obvious that I was not like other kids. I already knew how to read all the books that were in that year's curriculum. With math, I just saw the answer with my mind like a photograph. It made me feel like an outsider. Why could I do this and no one else could? What was wrong with me? Intelligence did not seem like a blessing, but rather a curse. Just a few months into that year, I got a nasty case of the chickenpox. I was less upset about the itching than the fact I would be missing school. Even my grandma's daily presents while I was sick did not cheer me up. So my teacher gave me these workbooks, one for math and one for reading. She gave me assignments so I could stay up to date, but instead I just did both books start to finish during my two week contagious spell. After that I got moved to first grade to finish out the year. Then I skipped second grade and went straight to third. Even though my parents insisted that I still have gym and recess with kids my age, those years were difficult when it came to making friends. Follow couldn't even cheer me up. I was lonely.

In the first grade, I had this teacher called Ms. Clark. She was new and younger than the rest of the teachers. She tried to wear the brightest, shiny blue eye shadow available. She wore leggings combined with various baggy sweatshirts that all had school themes. One of them was covered with different colored pencils and apples floating together. I was sure she used a whole can of Aqua Net on her bangs each morning. She tried at first to be as cool as we thought we were, but it was awkward. Even then I could feel the tension. One day after class while all the kids were trickling out of the room to the buses she asked me to sit on her lap because we needed to have a talk.

I was searching my brain. I couldn't think of anything I had ever done wrong at school. What was this about? She explained to me that I was not hanging out with the cool kids enough. She said I was only sticking to my particular group of friends. What's wrong with that? I didn't understand. She said that I was being rude. Didn't she realize that it wasn't me? The cool kids didn't want to hang out with me with my glasses and nerdy appearance. I cried and cried. I felt so misunderstood. She just smiled at me, I got up and she tapped me on the bum. "Everything will be alright from now on, right? Right?" I didn't even look back. I now hated her. I wasn't going to have anyone tell me who I could and could not be friends with. It never made sense to me what she was trying to accomplish besides being a bully herself. At that time, I was pretty social for me at least. It wasn't like I just was by myself thinking I was better than everyone else. I told my parents. And that was when I switched into third grade with a new, much more understanding teacher.

The best thing Scarborough Public School System had to offer was to separate me from the rest of my class. I had to sit in the corner with this one other smart boy named Tom Hendrix and spend the day taking placement tests with some Educational Technician. The goal was to move me into the eighth grade, which was where they believed I was intellectually. I was only seven. The differences between seven and thirteen year olds are drastic in many ways including physically, emotionally, and sexually. The eight graders weren't exactly going to play with a rock tumbler, Barbie, or Matchbox cars. No one would play dress up with me. I wasn't use to being preoccupied with my physical appearance. I didn't wonder if I looked good or bad. All I saw when I looked in the mirror was someone beautiful. I really didn't care what anyone else thought. At that time, I didn't realize that this self-confidence wouldn't stay so strong later in life.

Now conversations that buzzed around me centered on clothing, music, and boys. All things I did not care about yet. Some girl named Tasha gave me a New Kids On The Block pin for my backpack to help me be cool. She told me to pick which one of the boys I thought was hot and practice kissing him on my pillow at night. Kiss my pillow? How bizarre. I didn't know what to do. It seemed completely out of my hands. I felt like I was being punished for being smart. Next year I would try my best to be slow.

But then my third grade teacher Mr. Jenkins suggested that I switch to Waynflete, a co-ed private school in Portland. I would still remain one grade ahead but otherwise I would not have to change grades anymore. He said it was quite expensive but there was a chance that they would give me a scholarship. So I went for a visit, which I had no idea meant eight hours of placement tests. I have always liked tests so I sat at a desk and took them one after another.

I had my lunch break with the other students close to my age. I asked if this was a hard school. It is definitely different then public school, they said. The biggest difference was that there weren't any classes bigger then five children. If you don't do your homework and spend the assigned amount of study time they will know. This place is made for success. I asked if most people had to take tests, like me, when they applied. They all shook their head no. I quickly realized that this school was for rich kids that did well in school because of the constant one to one attention. No one was left behind.

There was also the very important Honor Code. Once signed it meant that you would never cheat on any test or other assignment or even receive help other that just studying facts as a group. When we had a test the teacher would leave the room. In all the years that followed, no one ever tried anything. No one ever made a joke. There were no cheat sheets or details written in the palm of someone's hand. If you caught someone breaking the honor code you were to tell the Dean of Students immediately and they would be removed from the school. If you knew of such a malfeasance and did not report it you would be held under the same penalty.

This intense honor code kept any one from ever messing up. There was no teasing, bullying, or hate crimes of various natures. There was no such thing as detention, suspension, and expulsion. If you got caught skipping, they figured you were already paying the price from missing out on your own education. If someone did drugs on campus, their parents would buy a new wing for the library or a gym. Everything was strictly kept quiet and under the table. You didn't even have to wear shoes if you didn't want to. I guess some people may say that we were spoiled but it never felt that way. I felt free to do, think, and believe anything I wanted. I felt like the school trusted our judgment, which was so important. At Gorham High School my cousin got caught for wearing a t-shirt with an ad for Trojan Condoms on it. He was suspended for a week. Needless to say I was glad I didn't have to deal with that bullshit.

After taking the placement tests for the forth grade (I was supposed to be in the second) it was determined that this school would be highly beneficial for me. I assumed that the faculty probably was hopeful that my placement there would be beneficial for Waynflete School's name. Each full year of courses cost approximately twelve thousand dollars give or take. The price went up each year as the courses became more intensive and the professors were required to have the terminal degree in their field. I had no idea why I was even visiting and taking all these tests considering we bought brand name toilet paper and milk for home. But thanks to my grades and IQ, I was immediately offered a full scholarship. The Dean of Students said as long as I maintained having straight A's that I would be given my scholarship each year. He made it clear that even an A minus would not be acceptable. This all seemed like a lot of pressure. What if I messed up, just once, would I loose everything? Will I be able to make friends or will they treat me like a dork? Should I get rid of my glasses? How long could I keep the fact that I was on scholarship a secret? All my fears and questions quickly dissipated and I realized I was right where I belonged and that getting good grades was achievable.

Waynflete is a private school. It isn't a boarding school. Of course there have been many changes since I was there. Back in my day, you went back and forth to school every day just like any other school. The campus is spread out like a college so you have ten minutes in between classes to walk to your next course because it might be in another building across campus. There were no lockers just heavy LLBean backpacks. The days were much longer than public school, but to make up for it every Wednesday was half a day. When I first started there were twenty-two students in my class. Only nine of them were male. Much later on when we entered high school we had a big increase in the student body because parents wanted their child to graduate from a prestigious school even if they couldn't afford it the other years. Our class, the class of 2000, was forty-six students; nineteen male and twenty-seven female.

I had a group of friends that I was close to from the beginning all the way through. Three of them I was particularly close to. For a long time it was always the four of us doing everything together. I had thought that I would miss my old friends terribly and I didn't want to go to such a new, scary place, but this is not how it went at all. I quickly realized that I didn't really have any true friends at my previous school. I was ready to have true substantial relationships. Slowly over the years my group of friends got larger as more students joined the school at the beginning to middle school and high school. I was always in the most advanced courses; getting anything other than an A was not an option. The need to have perfect grades was imposed by me, not my parents. Silly when you are so young, but that was the kind of kid I was. The thought of getting kicked out mortified me in more ways than one. I was mostly into math and science. I progressed so quickly that I was taking advanced calculus my freshman year of high school.

Neither my mother nor my father had ever even mentioned God or the idea of religion. It was as if the concept completely didn't exist in my life. If I believed in anything it was the power of Mother Nature. The fact I missed all of this made for some difficulties with some kids at school. At some point a few months into starting the fourth grade I asked my dad what it meant to be religious. He told me that there are many different types of religion but they were all basically the same. They were all based on a series of stories that were written to make people feel better about things that they felt guilty about and to not be afraid of death. He told me it was nothing I needed to bother myself with. He said I didn't need other people's stories to figure out my life because I was smart enough to figure it out all on my own.

After this talk, I pretty much thought of Santa Clause as the equivalent of God because they both were fictitious stories to make people feel good. So far in my life the topic had never been brought up and to this day I have never once been to a church service. The idea of believing that some mythic figure as real to me as the Easter bunny was in charge of all life on earth seemed not just bizarre but crazy. It wasn't that I was narrow minded I just didn't know what they were talking about. At the time, I didn't realize this could be offensive.

I immediately became very close with my new friend Jen. She was a very school orientated and we were usually in every class together. She had been to my house a few times but I had never been to hers yet. She asked me to stay overnight and I was very excited. When we sat down together for dinner they all put out their hands so we could hold each other in a circle. I thought it was weird they wanted to hold my hand since this was my first time there and I wasn't part of their family. But they grabbed my hands tightly, so much so that I couldn't escape their grip. It felt like silent threat as if I tired to let go that something bad would happen. Jen's father asked me if I would lead the Lord's Prayer. As politely as I could I said, "I'm sorry. I don't believe in God. May I be excused?" I was totally freaked out. Surely I am trapped in some kind of cult, I thought. And I ran down stairs into their basement before they even replied. About ten minutes later Jen came downstairs. I apologized for leaving the table. She told me the damage was already done and her parents weren't going to have "a sinner like myself in the their house anymore." They had already called my parents to come and get me. I didn't understand why we couldn't just all believe what we personally wanted and still have a nice dinner together. My parents picked me up and didn't say one word all the way home.

After some interesting research, I found that in conclusion, there is enough evidence on the Internet to support the statement that individuals that are more educated are associated with less belief in God. A possibility to why educated people seem to have a lower level of religiosity is that they are less likely to believe ideas if no actual proof is presented to them. With people who are not highly educated, they seem to turn to religion to provide them with explanations for the unknowns in their lives.

My real passion throughout the years had always been dancing. It always came number one on my list. First it was just tap and ballet, but then I added Pointe, lyrical, jazz, hip-hop, clogging and contemporary. After I got done school every day I would go straight to the dance studio, change, and begin working hard for about four hours on weekdays and six hours on weekends. Because I was being so active, I was able to get my gym time revoked from my school day so I could spend more time dancing.

When you first get a new pair of Pointe shoes there is a ritual of sorts to make them comfortable, safe, and wearable. The sole of a new shoe is one hard piece of wood making it impossible to use the arch of your foot for balance and pointing your foot unless you break them in. You spend hours bending it in half where your arch hits. Back and forth for hours until it feels like rubber. Some people even put half their shoe in the door jam and slam the door shut to help get the proper fitting. If you don't do this correctly, it can cause the wooden sole to snap unexpectedly which will cause a sprained ankle. Next, you need to cut of the pretty satin from the toe of the shoe, the part you dance on top of, with a razor blade for increased traction. You have to then burn the edges so the rest of the shoe stays in tack. Lastly, you must scratch up the wooden sole of the shoe so you don't slip. This all may sound ridiculous. I mean you basically have to wreck a brand new shoe, but it is for the best. If you see someone who hasn't done this, and is so proud of their pretty, new shoes, you know they're green.

My favorite style by far was tap. I just had a precise sense of timing. I got to the point where I couldn't even sit still without taping with my feet at the table. Most people don't know that tappers must keep their legs slightly bent and their heels off the ground at all times unless the heel is necessary for a particular sound. You get very good at always walking with your heels just off the ground. I can still do this for hours at a time even now. I guess some things don't go away. All my other training in other types of dance brought me to a whole other level with my tapping. Within the group of us that got chosen to go to competition, I was easily the fastest learner. I could be shown a dance just once and repeat it accurately. I just pictured it in my mind.

Preparing for dance competitions became my focus. I kind of kept it a secret to my friends at school. Most of them didn't even know I could dance until they came over to my house and saw all my awards and pictures. I wanted it to be my thing. It was what I was the best at. I wanted it to be mine. Many years before American Idol or other reality TV talent competitions existed there was a whole other world. There were no goofy famous judges that didn't have any dancing background. I went to competitions in New York City, Boston, Atlanta, and even Italy for three months to dance with the Perugia Dance Company. We went to the most prestigious dance competitions in the country. To get there we had already been through at least five previous rounds of judging to help narrow down who got to go to the finale. Plus the judges, agents from movies, commercials, print ads, and professional dance companies would be watching. At the end, if your name was on the board you knew you were picked from some amazing job or audition.

But all this came second to me, I really didn't care about being in a Barbie commercial. One year they wanted me to be part of some new Nickelodeon show called Clarissa Explains It All to play the friend of the main character for a few episodes. I didn't want to miss school so I declined. Plus, even though I wouldn't admit it, the whole idea made me nervous. I just wanted to dance, dance, dance. My dance team almost always won and rarely came in second place. Slowly, my parents didn't care anymore. I would come home so excited but there was no reaction to my achievements, which squashed my happiness and confidence. I felt like my accomplishments bored them.

~ Three ~

Everyday I would sit on the filthy wooden dance floor put on my Pointe shoes and wrap dirty wool around and in between each bloody toe. Despite all the pain it felt worth it. One afternoon out of the corner of my eye, I saw my mother showing off this book with photographs of young girls I didn't know to the other mothers in the waiting room. The women's collective sign song tone of voice made it sound like they were shopping for a new pair of high heels. "Oh, look at the porcelain tone of her skin." "Oh, no, not that one. Everyone will think you are married to a Black." "How much does this one cost?" Could I actually be hearing this correctly? Was this a book of children for sale to bored white mothers?

Okay, so my first judgment was a little harsh but I wasn't totally wrong either. My mother had brought a five-inch binder with photos and brief descriptions of children up for adoption from the Department of Heath and Human Services. It seemed like by showing this book off to other mothers made her look and feel like a true philanthropists. Her sudden desire to adopt another child was a decision she made without speaking to my father or myself. Since she physically couldn't have any more children this was the next best way to find yet another thing she could control and possess now that I was starting to become more independent. Dad said, "Sara, someday you will learn. You can never stop what your mother wants." "Daddy, what is mom's word?" "Manipulative," he quickly responded.

But then again, I never saw them fight, have a small argument, or disagree. You're thinking weird, right? It was peculiar. Maybe once a month they would both go in their bedroom together and lock the door. I always figured they were having sex, but I was so far off. They were fighting in the quietest possible way. I assume they did it to protect me. It was a good thing I had my grandparents relationship as a model.

All dad and I heard during that time was, "Oh your mother is such a wonderful care giver. She wants to save the world." As if she was some fucking Mother Theresa. She would tell them stories of all these achievements that I had were completely made up. Then they would pinch my cheek and tell me how excited I was to have two new sisters. My mother had probably integrated that falsehood during her speeches of being the perfect mother. But what they didn't know was that all my mother wanted to do was save herself. To remain in control. A selfish bitch. There are many people in this world that are considered "bad" but they are suffering and they need help. They are good inside. But I firmly believe there are just a few people out there with black hearts. My mother is one of them. No one ever asked me if I wanted a sibling. I would overhear fictional conversations explaining how I was lonely and I desperately wanted a sister to play with. That I had begged her to give me another sister. I always knew where the lies were coming from. This wasn't hearsay. They were coming directly out of her mouth. Besides my mother, I didn't know anyone else that would be spilling so many falsities. Unfortunately, everything got very out of control.

And then suddenly they appeared. I was seven, Crystal was six, and Joanna was four. They had been in the foster system their entire lives. Passed from one abusive home to the next. They were repeatedly made to witness others being abused, forced to take it all in, waiting for their chance to do it themselves and take charge. Rather than despising those who abused them they looked up to them. They wanted to play God too. Sadly, they were abused in all the worst ways. Hammers, belts, clothes ripped off while the rest of the girls watched as the dad of the moment finished the last swig from his Pabst Blue Ribbon. All the time this sick fuck is thinking that THIS is what video cameras were made for.

Of course, none of the information about their abuse and other severe residual behaviors was even hinted at in their little blurb in the adoption binder. Their description was listed with a small picture with misfitting clothing and a forced smile. "She likes to play with dolls and ride her bike." Or "Very social, loves to play board games and draws pictures." "Enjoys singing and playing with animals." Every girls supposedly personalized sentence was just as interchangeable as the next. How did you know whom to pick? You look into their eyes and it's all the same; shame and loneliness.

We had several different girls come over for a trial visit for the afternoon. It just never felt right. One girl told me that she wanted to cut my hair off and wear it. Another said she didn't like dogs but she knew how to "take care of that problem." But then again, even from the beginning, Crystal and Joanna weren't quite right either. I knew from the beginning they were not close to normal and it wasn't because they were mildly retarded either, which didn't phase me in the least. The truth is that I was used to people being a little slower than me. I never minded explaining things to people. Sometimes, I even enjoyed it. I could tell that there was something that was just wrong about these two. Especially Joanna, the younger one, she was much smarter than Crystal and looked at me like I was her only prey in the desert. She was a four-year-old intellectual psychopath. At first, mom had decided to only adopt one child but because they were sisters my mother couldn't help get both. I mean how could she ever separate two medically insane children from abusing her only biological child.

Since my room was so big my parents moved us all up there together. At first I tried. I really tried to make it work. Teaching them things they had never had the opportunity to experience. I would try to play games with them, but everything always had a twisted way about. One day when we were playing Candy Land every time Crystal got a card that moved her backward she would remove a piece of clothing. When I asked her what she was doing she just said Joanna likes it that way. During dress up one day they demanded to see me naked. Joanna pulled out selection of kitchen knives she had snuck from the kitchen and collected them underneath her pillow. She puffed up her chest to show how proud she was of her compilation. When I said no they told me they would show me how to do it and they tried to take my clothes off. All with the collection of knives sitting there threatening me. I screamed and yelled but my parents were outside. After Joanna told me, "Don't you dare tell Mama okay because that will be the end. I will kill her, then Daddy, so you can watch, and then you will be my masterpiece".

What young child says masterpiece anyway?

I couldn't believe two children younger than I was could have such control over me and manipulate me in so many ways. I was so afraid sometimes I felt paralyzed. I couldn't get out of the situation. I think it was because there were two of them with the same mind set and they worked together. Just sitting in the same room as them gave me goose bumps. It made me feel like something must be wrong with me because I couldn't make it stop.

They caused other problems too. One day when I woke up it was dark and I couldn't breath. When I pushed against the blackness all I could hear was the crinkle of plastic. My chest felt so heavy. I was gasping for air. I could feel myself starting to black out. Things were getting so dark in my mind. While I was sleeping both girls had taken trash bags, put them over my head and synched them tightly around my neck. Joanna sat on my chest while Crystal kept the trash bags shut. They had duct taped my wrists together. I could hardly breath. Crystal held on so tight to the garbage bag strings and I was running out of air so much I could barely yell. I became sure that this was the end. My dad thought it was weird I hadn't come downstairs yet for school and he found me. He swatted the girls away like flies and tore open the bag around my face so I could breath. He told my mother it was enough and they needed to leave.

"You let those little shits into our house and now they have threatened Sara's life on more than one occasion. What are you waiting for? Where is your fucking limit, Pam? If nothing changes then I am making a change. Sara and I are moving out of here. You can be left to disintegrate on your own." I wanted so much for this to be true. Unfortunately, this was only talk. I never quite understood what kept him from making a move. I knew he didn't approve the situation, he didn't love my mother and money wasn't an issue. The house was actually only in his name so he could have even kicked her out. What was the problem? I knew he loved me. I guess he was scared of change. Maybe his mental illness made things just too hard to take a hold of and make a move. But for him just to speak up meant so much to me. It was almost enough.

As always she took the "But I can fix them. They just need the right things in their life. I can change them" defense. Did she actually believe she could save these two girls or did she just like to say it so other people would believe that she was kind and generous and could save the world?

I was hoping that Dad was mad enough to runaway with me. I would dream at night that we would run away together to Grenada, his favorite place. But that's all that it was, a dream. Confrontation just wasn't his way. My parents had to sleep with their door locked every night because one evening Joanna came at them with a knife in their sleep. But yet, they weren't scared of me sleeping upstairs with them night after night. They never ever asked me if I was okay. Where did the bite mark on my shoulder come from?

When I would get checked for my yearly physical with my

pediatrician he was always full of questions. Where did all these bruises and scrapes come from? Even from frequently visiting the emergency room there were questions. My mother would pretend to look calm, cool, and confused blaming it all on the fact I was a klutz. But all her stories just weren't believable The doctor would say that the adopted girls had to go if she had any hope of saving her own daughter from serious bodily injury. When we walked out into the parking lot together she quickly spit out, "He doesn't know what he is talking about." And would throw the discharge papers on the sidewalk. This struck me as amusing because he had been my doctor since birth and in the past she had said he was the only doctor she could trust. But that was just the thing; she didn't know anything about trust.

What really ended it all was when we got this cute, little kitten I called Kevin. Someone had dropped him off in a basket at our front door with a note saying they "couldn't take care of him and to please give him a good life". We had to bottle-feed him for weeks because he hadn't been ready to leave his mother yet. He was fragile and quiet. A month later, I remember Kevin lying on the floor playing with a toy mouse and my mother commented how lucky we were to have him. She held him for just a moment and went to her bedroom just in time for Days of Our Lives, which she always watched laying in bed with a bag of Hershey kisses. Joanna took her fingers and ripped both his eyeballs out of his head in one swift motion as if she was cleaning out a sea urchin. She walked down the hall leisurely holding the running jelly of Kevin's eyeballs to my mother and said, "See, mommy, now he can't look at you anymore", in the calmest and happiest tone of voice I had ever heard from her. We had to have Kevin put to sleep that same afternoon.

In about a week, Joanna and Crystal were transferred to a long-term psychiatric hospital in Vermont. Joanna went first. Crystal two days later. I think my mother would have benefitted from attending the family program that focused on enabling. She was a grieving mess and my father just kept saying how glad he was that those children were gone. He believed they were possessed. When Mom would cry, Dad (who never raised his voice) would yell, "Stop it! Stop It! You are forgetting that we are even here." Mom believed she could have fixed them if she had more time. Emotions of all kinds were running wild. I had nightmares of all sorts. Both real and imaginative things were happening to me.

At some point after they left dad shamefully whispered, "I'm sorry you had to put up with all that. You never deserved to be treated like crap." I felt like a weight had been lifted off my shoulders. It is amazing how two little sentences could mean so much.

And on the other side mom said, "You know, I don't think you ever even wanted to make things work with them. You were being selfish. This was supposed to be about me and not you. So what if they upset you sometimes. You should have dealt with it better." This just brought me back down. All this and I was just nine years old.

The time the two girls were with us almost seemed like a horror movie. I have tried to block so much out of my mind over the years. And even as I tell it now, I realize that I made it sound shorter than it was. This terror went on for over two years. During which I was suffocated, stabbed, hit, poked with a hot iron from the fireplace, and thrown down the stairs multiple times. What I remember the most though was when things got really bad my dad would tell me to go into my bathroom and lock the door until he said I could come out. I would hear yelling, but in a whisper, full of passion and intention. I never really knew what happened when I was in the bathroom lying on the cold white tiles. I tried to find some answers to it all but I just felt like I was drowning. We never talked about it. I just knew he was doing his best to keep me safe.

~ Four ~

About three months after the girls had left, my nervousness had just begun to fade, my father got back to his old routines, but my mother was a different story. She sunk into this hole of what could I have done, should I have done, could I have fixed it all? But that was the problem. No one could just fix it. Fixing was not an option. Maybe some facility could keep them from harming themselves or others, but that is far as it goes. There was no cure for what was wrong with them. Somewhere in that twisted mind of hers I know she knew that. She wanted to call and talk to them, visit them even, but a ban had been placed for safety reasons. We had to change our phone number, street number, even our last name and other personal information. The psychiatrists at the facility believed they both were a danger because they would repeat our information over and over again. They were afraid that if they were to escape that they would come directly for us. Even many years later they still remained a threat. My mother seemed to forget that I even existed. Depression overcame her entire being. She had no reason to live it seemed. It was time of intense emotions for all of us.

And it was at this time I had made up my mind to end my life. The decision to commit suicide is never an impulsive one. If it seems that way you won't follow through. Just harming yourself is a completely different concept. Suicide is a decision that you make over and over again before attempting anything. Every time you feel depressed, uncertain, lonely, or fearful you make the decision to end it all again and again and again. To me no one cared about my existence, let alone my happiness, and I had become a huge burden to my grandparents. After my parents went to sleep, I slit my throat.

Somehow I missed the carotid artery. I passed out almost immediately. My parents didn't check on me before they left the house that morning and when my grandfather came to pick me up for school he found me and was able to wake me up a little. He brought me to his house and stitched up my wound with a sharp needle made for sewing leather shoes. He began to clean and bandage my wounds. The whole time quietly telling me to never ever mention this to anyone, especially my parents. He didn't judge me for what I had done. I think somewhere deep down he understood why I had done it. He cleaned me off and tucked me into bed. I went to school four days later and we pretended I had been going the whole time. I wore turtle necks for weeks. My parents have never known anything about that incident.

We never spoke about it again.

Dad always did all the grocery shopping and the cooking. I loved going with him on Saturday mornings to get the weeks worth of food at Shop 'n Save leaving just enough money for his weekly one carton of Camels. He budgeted so well that the bill would come to close to the same dollar every week. He seemed to enjoy it for the most part. We had a beautiful mahogany dining room table but we never ate there together once. It was where I did my homework and my dad paid the bills. We either ate at separate times and places or all in the living room.

This night was like any other. Dad had cooked the two of them pork chops, and green beans something I despised. The smell of the can of green beans opening was directly associated with the way I detested my mother. I had cereal and a piece of fruit. We were watching Rosanne in our separate chairs. So it must have been around 7:30pm. I remember my mother dropped her fork onto the floor and when she rose back to sitting the entire left side of her face was sliding down towards the floor. Her left arm moved up into a clutched position at her chest and she was speaking nonsense. It was hard to believe that this had all happened so fast. There was no time for 911. The three of us got in the car and dad dropped me off at his parents on the way and said I needed to spend the night. They took one look at mom and didn't ask any questions. My grandparents brought me inside for angel cake and strawberries. None of us had any idea at that moment how serious all this was to become. My dad drove straight to Maine Medical Center.

The next day I saw her and she had no idea who I was or even who she was. She couldn't speak, read, or write. An aneurysm had burst in the lower part of her brain causing a severe stroke. The doctors were surprised she was alive. Her face was still disfigured and her left leg was not working at all. They told us she would never walk again. She was only thirty-six years old.

During this unstable time, I would go to school, then dance for only two to three hours, so I could visit mom while I did my homework. I then spent the rest of the time with my grandparents because my dad had to work overtime now that mom couldn't work and there were so many medical bills. I missed dad during this time, but I understood what he had to do. I wondered if my presence even mattered to her. It seemed like she wasn't even there. As if her body was the only part of her that remained. She didn't even look at me. The doctors insisted that she could hear me, but I think they just didn't want me to feel alone.

This was when my grandmother taught me how to knit. I knew that our relationship had moved to a new place when she showed me her most precious item. Her hope chest was made by my grandfather for her engagement present to put all her most sacred items when she moved in with him. It was the only thing of hers that I hoped I would get to hold on to for the rest of my life. It is the most treasured material possession I could ever dream of. The hope chest is a special item to put in my home that holds the history of my blood.

Hidden like a child in a ghost costume underneath the cloth, the trunk waits to be discovered for the first time in six years. Six years since it was last touched, and now it has fallen apart, blossomed past its peak. I reached out and within and fingered an old bouquet that rests surrounded by broken petals. The petals felt like grandmothers skin on the top of her hand. My grandmother's hand that felt like a puppets hand, when you can feel the wires underneath the cloth. The cloth over the top of the trunk hadn't been touched in six years. I touch the embroidery on the blanket inside, letting my hand linger, leaving my fingers laying on the pink lace on the pillowcase, and looking at the print of the petals. It reminds me of grandmother knitting and her own delicate hands, the color of sand. The cloth that once was the nightgown that she wore for six years. The nightgown that would always calm her worst fears, that was so much a part of us for years. Just like the bouquet that has now come apart against grandmothers wedding dress and gloves. I thought that someday my whole hand will be transformed just like grandmothers to feel like delicate rose petals and I will wear the nightgown her hands made me from the cloth, and in sixty years the trunk will sit in my room with my baby cloth. A cloth of my own, a perfect touch, a perfect smell that will smell of petals, my own petals that have danced and fallen apart on the tops of my hands.

Mom stayed in the long-term wing at the hospital for almost a year. She had a roommate with close to the same problem. Over time she began to speak but she wouldn't make sense. She would say, "light bulb bumblebee" which I later learned meant, "pass the butter". Or "Blow out the candle" which meant "Shut up". I felt like dad and I had to learn a whole other language. She started to use a brace on her left leg with canes, which allowed for a few steps and then falls that resulted in broken bones. At the time, I despised her for not working harder. If the physical trainer said she could do it then why was she playing the victim? And this was all called, "progress". But she quickly became worse again in more ways than one. She began developing tonic-colonic seizures that would cause her to have super human strength. During one of her episodes she could bend and then break the metal bars on the hospital bed.

During this time, I began to face having surgery. Seeing my mother making no progress for years scared me to do anything about my condition even though what I had was very different. I was born with an unusual birthmark. If you bend your chin down to your chest, where your chin hits is exactly were it was. It was the size of a quarter and had dark rings like the inside of a tree. The weirdest part was that when I would tighten the muscles in my neck the middle of it would pucker up and rise in the shape of a peanut. When I was little I thought it was a cool trick. I loved to show everyone. But I never could find a doctor that had any idea what it was until I was eleven years old. I went to a plastic surgeon and he said it was a ring muscle that for some reason was on the outside of my skin rather than deep inside my body. He thought that because it was exactly in the middle of my chest that I was meant to separate, to be two babies. Twins.

Because it wasn't just a mole or something only on the surface it wasn't exactly easy to remove. This mark was attached by one cord to my sternum and another to my left rib. He told me he would have to make two twelve inch cuts. One straight down the middle of my chest. And the other across my left breast. This was devastating for a girl nearing puberty. How ugly was I to become? Would my left breast be disfigured? Who would ever accept me for who I was to become? The only reason I had to do this was because the cords were only so long and they were preventing me from growing properly and were starting to cause pain. More importantly, it would eventually cause difficulties with breathing.

Despite the seriousness and uniqueness of the surgery they said it would only take the day and then I could go home. I went under anesthesia without knowing what was about to happen. For some reason during the operation I stopped breathing, and they had to defibrillate. But the anesthesiologist put an adult tube instead of a child's down my mouth and he put it into my esophagus instead of my windpipe. The entire contents in my stomach flooded into my lungs and one of them collapsed. When I woke up I had no idea what had happened and my parents were only told that I had hard time breathing and it was easily fixed. The anesthesiologist told me that I was fine to head home right away in a panic to avoid blame. He was the one that was supposed to make that call.

So I went home, laid down, and within fifteen minutes I started turning blue. I could barely breath. My left lung was still collapsed. I was rushed to the hospital and went immediately in the trauma room. They kept telling me to sit up because they thought I just had a mole removed. They didn't realize that I had all my chest muscles cut in half and therefore there was no way I could sit up no matter what they said. I had an overload of bacteria in my body, a collapsed lung, and advanced pneumonia. They kept me in the hospital for four weeks.

The good thing is that I only ended up with a small two-inch scar where the mark had originally been instead. At least I wouldn't be as ugly as I had anticipated, but at the time it felt difficult to appreciate when I was nearly killed.

~ Five ~

Around the end middle school because of my various injuries I just sat, watched, and listened. It was around this time I got my first two CD's and a new boom box. I played Mariah Carey and Alanis Morissette repetitively and knew all the lyrics by heart. I couldn't carry a tune no matter how hard I tried, but I could memorize all the lyrics after only hearing the song once. People would talk about how

CD's would be a failure like the A-Trak and would advise not to buy into new technologies. I remember watching a lot of the OJ Simpson murder trial of 1995. It was so big in the media that we watched the verdict that October during biology class. We all had to place a bet on what we thought would happen. To me, it was definitely a moment in time that I will always remember. Some probably remember the president getting shot or the space shuttle exploding, but for me it was the fate of O.J. Simpson.

My grandparents were best friends with this couple Bea and Jim Ott. At least twice a week they would get together, go out for dinner, and then go back to one of their houses to play pinochle for a few hours. They had all known each other almost their whole lives. The Ott's were the type of people that always saw the bright side of life and it wasn't all show either. They were happy and always had been. Jim eyes always twinkled. They were the perfect double dating couple. Always telling some big story that just made them laugh and laugh. They weren't family by blood but to me they are my family and always have been.

Pinochle is usually played with four people; two teams of two or it can be played with six but that's rare. When I got old enough I would go out to eat with them and watch them play cards. Once I was good enough, I learned how to keep score. It was always the girls versus the boys. When my grandmother passed away I took her place and was Bea's new partner against the boys. Most of my friends would laugh at me or think I was joking. Why was a teenager playing pinochle with her grandparents twice a week? But it was the most fun, supportive, and creative time I had. When Jim died his daughter Sue took his place and she played with Grandpa. But then once Grandpa died the pinochle days ended. Bea, Sue, and I still go out for lunch every once in a while to catch up. I truly do miss them. The good old times.

My grandma developed pneumonia at Christmas time and by Valentines Day she had passed away. One night my mother came home from visiting her at the hospital. She busted through the front door saying that she has something to tell me. But her pee pee dance made her unable to tell me anything. She frantically waved her hand for me to follow her. She ran into my bathroom pulled her pants half down and let out a sigh of relief as she let it loose like a horse. Unfortunately, I remember this image perfectly. She showed no sadness and said, "Uh, so she just died tonight. Wow! I really thought I was going to pee my pants." Who the hell cares about your piss when the most important woman in my life just died so suddenly?

The rest of my eighth grade year was full of grief. Only made worse by my mother telling me I had no right to be as upset as I was. According to her I was overreacting. One day I was in a rage. I despised her. Out came, "Fuck you. She was my mother. I bet you arranged all this."

At my annual dance recital that year, I looked out into the audience during a performance and saw Follow. She was lying on the carpet in the aisle. I wanted to believe that she was there. I was lonely. I needed her and she came back to me.

I knew I needed to be there for my grandfather. I had to be strong. It happened so quickly my grandfather was in shock. He would only speak to me for at least two months. I was the only one that knew how he felt. We spent every day together. I have never been closer to anyone in my life. And in all the years that followed, it was always me and him. We both had each other's back. There were no lies. No unnecessary conversation. We didn't even need to talk sometimes. We just knew what each other were thinking. We were both so overcome with tragedy we bonded together as one.

I tried to remain busy to keep my mind off the grief surrounding me. In general I didn't watch much TV. I didn't play video games. I would go to dance class to watch, coach, choreograph, and try to learn. There were other distractions staring to pop up. There was this high school sophomore her name was Erica. Erica Sanders. She was older and better than I was so she had a solo routine that she was practicing for the next competition. She was driven and passionate, two qualities that I admired. She was wearing this low cut leotard with a v-shaped back. She danced to Bryan Adams' Run to You. Her legs were so strong and smooth. She didn't spray her dark hair back like the rest of us; she let it flow wild over her shoulder blades. She danced with so much passion it almost felt like she was making love to me. For the first time in my life I felt the muscles in my vagina throb for thirty seconds or so. I wasn't even touching myself. It just happened. I felt like everyone knew and their eyes were all over me. But they had no idea about the private party between my thighs. I hoped that no one noticed, especially Erica. I had never felt that way about anyone, any boy. Even my inexperienced masturbation techniques never gave me that feeling. So what did this mean? I tried not to think about it. But I always waited anxiously for her next performance. My voice seemed to disappear when she would say hello. I would try to stand behind her when we practiced on the bar. And no, I was not a stalker. Come on, you weren't that different. Imagine all the creepy things you did when you were having your first crush.

I wondered if this was how my friends felt about boys. Or was this some special feeling? One thing was clear though, when my friends would be looking at a group of guys I would be looking at their girlfriends. I didn't tell anyone for fear my parents would kick me out and my friends would think that I was disturbing and that I would be prohibited from going over their houses anymore. I made up fake crushes with unattainable guys at school so no one would catch on. I picked this one guy named Alden. He had never even really had a conversation with me. He was the perfect choice. But it wasn't just that, I was hoping that if I pretended to like guys bodies that maybe I would change. Maybe I could be made normal. I was never trying to fool anyone. I just wanted to fit in. I wasn't lucky enough to be born normal. I never dated anyone from my school until just before graduation.

There was no way to pretend that this wasn't happening. I couldn't help it. Women are just so soft, sexy, and innocent. I had a craving to roll my fingers back and forth along a girl's nipple as she looked down and watched me. Their lips are so delicate that I would dream of placing mine on theirs. And to run my fingers through their hair, sink my hands into the small of their back, and pull them in tight until they let out a small whispering gasp. When my eyes were pulled towards a girl, it just felt right. I wasn't hurting anyone. Isn't that all that should matter?

Did this make me sick? I never thought so, but I knew other people did. Just as a friend made what they thought was an innocent joke it always took a little piece of me away. "Look at her, she's so fucking gay." The comments ate away at me piece by piece. I had to put up Leonardo DiCaprio and Matt Damon posters on my walls to confuse those around me. I knew all the right comments to make about their abs and how big their cock probably was. I didn't want to be a liar. I really didn't want people to think all those years I had been faking it so I could get close to my girlfriends bodies when they changed into their pajamas at my house. I wasn't a pervert. Just because I like women doesn't mean I want all of them. And no, it doesn't mean that I get turned on when I look in the mirror.

Throughout this time I continued dancing excessively which led to winning competition after competition. My dance instructor had thin, black, frizzy hair that was like a white woman's Afro. Her name was Gail. She had been a successful dancer early in life but with age she decided to move into choreography and opened her own dance center. She actually lived four houses up the street from me. I saw her all the time. Who knew some dance center in the middle of nowhere could help us girl's to reach so far? I even got a spot on Star Search, the original TV talent competition, which we lost because someone dropped someone's foot on the floor. How on earth could this have happened we had been practicing everyday for months? But it was an accomplishment nonetheless. I also got asked to be part of the Radio City Rockettes. I was the exact height and size they were looking for at the time. I made it to the final round of the audition process but then I got cut. I felt sad at first, but now that I think about it I was just embarrassed. The truth was I couldn't handle the expectation to all be the same, same weight, same height, eat the same, and act the same. Because at that time, I had never felt more different than every one else. At fourteen, I received the honor of being part of the National Dance Choreographer Society. I was a back up dancer for many singing groups at the time. I was a great dancer. But then it all started to fall apart.

Because of the excessive dancing six to seven hours a day, I began to develop severe stress fractures in both legs multiple times over the last years. My tibia and fibula were cracked repeatedly. At first, I just thought it was pain from dancing too much. At certain point I had done so much damage that I had casts on both my lower legs. When I first started complaining from pain my mother told me I just had shin splints. She would repeat that everyone has some pain and that I should try and think of good thoughts. She might as well have told me to pray. It would have been completely worthless. Six months later I finally got an appointment with my doctor. By then, I had three stress fractures in my left leg. A lift had to be installed in the stairwell at my school so I could attend my classes. Even after my legs got better they were very susceptible to reoccurrences. My dance career spiraled rapidly down hill. It seemed like I was the only one who cared. People would say you will get too old to dance soon anyway. What a joke. I was only halfway through high school. No one gave a fuck. It is just dancing anyway. It was just my life, right? Now I sit on my ass and watch So You Think You Can Dance.

As my dance career was falling apart, the only saving grace was that when I turned fifteen I decided I wanted to get my pilots license after attending a Flight Camp in Montgomery, Alabama. My grandpa sent me there as a birthday present. A fire was immediately ignited in my gut. I was hooked. When I had a half-day on Wednesdays and during the weekend I would fly as long as the weather was clear. Flight lessons are an expensive hobby. At that time, a one-hour lesson was a little over one hundred dollars to pay for the instructor, the rental, and gas. I started out flying a Cessna 152. It is a propeller plane with two seats one for the pilot and the other for the copilot. It is really all you need to start learning. Well, that and a pillow for me to sit on so I could see over the dashboard. I was barely five feet tall. You can't get your pilots license until you are sixteen but I spent next year learning so I could take my tests right on my next birthday. I was going to make sure I would be ready. Luckily, because I was a girl the state of Maine gave me a flying scholarship to pay for my lessons until I got my license. I would go about twice a week depending on the weather.

I loved it. Every time Tim, my instructor, would ask me to pick an airport to go to. We would fly there, eat at the airport, and fly back. We would also do these exercises called Touch and Go's, which basically means you take off and then box in for a landing, land, and then take off again before you have even stopped. You could do about ten of those in an hour. They were great practice for landing which is the hardest part about learning to fly. But my favorite thing by far was to turn the throttle all the way off while in the air and pitch the airplane as high as possible. This quickly makes the plane stall and it either leans right or left. You never know which way. Then the plane begins to spiral straight towards the ground. You have to count while all this was happening because each spin gets faster and tighter. If you spin more than three times you will definitely crash because there would be no way to pull out of it. So you count while going around to the ground one, two, three. And then you push the throttle in all the way, pull the stick back hard, and the plane immediately recovers.

It was my thing. Well, my new thing. No one else could do it or even understand what I was talking about except for my grandfather who was drafted into the air force during World War II. A subject he never wanted to discuss. His purple heart remained under his mattress. Unlike many veterans, who wanted the world to know their life story by placing their supposed achievements on their license plate, grandpa tried his best to never remember such a horrible time. He always wore tan work paints with a matching long sleeved shirt buttoned all the way up to his chin every single day, all year long. For my graduation, he wore a white shirt, vest and a tie. But this was the only exception. It was then I knew that it really meant something to him. I wondered for years and even teased him a bit because I didn't know why he dressed this way especially all summer long.

One day when I was a teenager he had just had a hernia

removed. I was helping him change for bed when I saw all the humiliation and shame that had built up inside of him all these decades. He had the scars from third degree chemical burns over sixty percent of this body. While in air the enemy flew over them and dumped highly flammable chemical liquid sending the plane spiraling to the ground and leaving him as the only survivor. He was found four days later dehydrated and full of infection. The only thing he had to eat or drink was one can of beans. He said he had to drink one of his dead friends blood to survive. I have no idea how he made it. But I knew it was too hard to discuss. I didn't need anymore of an explanation. It was far too hard for him. Once I got my pilot license I asked my grandfather if I could take him for a short ride over the coast and back. I had this intense fear that I was asking too much. But he was full of smiles and gladly went with me. Afterwards he patted me on the back, "Good job, Sara, real decent work." It is probably the best compliment I had ever received.

~ Six ~

My mother's side of the family was bigger than dad's, but it was a mess. A bunch of people pretending to love each other so they wouldn't feel lonely on birthdays, Easter, and Father's Day while they shoved food in their mouths, unzipped their pants, and moaned as they watched the game on TV. They wanted to feel like the perfect family. A perfect group of idiots. The only religious people were my

Great Grandparents who were Baptist. They went to church so they could feel like they would be free from going to hell. At the same time they wished the rest of the people in their lives, that they supposedly loved, would go to hell. No one else considered themselves to be anything or believed in anything but Wal-Mart and tractor-trailers. When I was young I really enjoyed the company of my cousins. Following in the footsteps of their parents, my mothers two sisters abused and neglected my cousins. Luckily, the one right thing my mother ever did was to never ever lay a hand on me. I found out my aunt was doing more than just yelling at her kids if they did something she determined as bad. She took things way too far.

One Christmas, I hadn't seen Matthew running around in quite sometime. He was quiet, about five, and with over thirty people packed in the log cabin it was easy to miss someone for a little while. But what I found was beyond shocking. I was fifteen at the time. The bathroom door was shut so I knocked. There was no response but the door was locked. I could smell this strong odor of bleach or ammonia wafting from underneath the door. I heard whimpering so I kicked the door in to find Matt lying limp on the bathroom floor. My adrenaline was rushing and I had new found strength. I started screaming, "Someone help me. He's not breathing." My desperation got louder and louder. No one was helping me. I was told to mind my own business. The tub was filled with bleach and the windows were bolted shut too high for him to reach. He couldn't open the door because his hands had been tied together behind his back with duck tape along with a little over his mouth. I opened the window, ripped the tape off of his mouth, and ran to call 911. Smelling in the toxic fumes from the bathroom left him with permanent brain damage. The paramedics said that if I hadn't found him and called 911 that he had about fifteen minutes left. My aunt claimed he had said the F word so he "got what he deserved." I wrote a formal report to put along with the police report and gave it to Health and Human Services. All four of her children were taken away within a week. My parents took the two older siblings and the other two went to their fathers.

My whole mother's side of the family, each and every one of them, blamed me for tearing up the family. That this was a family matter and could have been dealt with differently. The whole problem was that each generation had abused the following one for many years. It had become acceptable. My aunt now played the victim because of what I had done and was facing prison charges. Now I would be the one that would suffer for what I had done to tear the family apart. They never wanted to see me again. I was disowned because I saved my cousin's life. I never felt guilty about it. I felt no regret. I was the devilish dyke home wrecker according to them. They couldn't risk being in my proximity just because my aura may send them to hell. After all this, dad and I stopped going to any family functions. We stayed home and did our own thing. When mom would go off to the latest and greatest family function Dad would yell out, "Have fun with the local Assholes!" The fact my mother kept going sealed another level of hatred inside of me. My hatred for her was like large onion that had grown foul smelling layers from each obsession and each manipulation that had occurred.

Mom was still recovering from her stroke and I was spending all my time after school with my grandfather. We were our own little family. We tried to have our own patterns, traditions, and structure that kept most fears from staying far away. Dance, homework, dinner, dessert, clean up, NBC Nightly News, all followed by Wheel of Fortune. Then Dad would take me home for the night.

In school, it was easy as usual. I craved for a change and it floated towards me like a butterfly. The Chewonki Foundation was for high school juniors to come and spend a challenging semester emphasizing the natural world, hands-on work, sustainability, and community. There were no parent visits, no television, no radio, no magazines, and definitely no Internet. The school just happened to be in Maine but I was the only student from here. Kids from top private schools across the country came to make the small group of thirty-six of us. I went during the spring semester.

Beneath the iridescent glow of the waning moon, I lay out stretched across the cold granite outcroppings of the point. As I felt the chill of the earth beneath me the biting wind passed over my head, the unsympathetic rock absorbed my heat, stealing my warmth and my comfort. Yet my concern was not this translation of heat but the stars that passed over as the earth's rotation coincided with their flight. My eyes were fixed upon the sky. In the black absence of sound and feeling, in the expanse of space, in the sea of scattered light and shattered rock my inquisitive eyes found a moment of solace. I was lost somehow, yet still fully aware of my cold back. A feeling of disconnection swept over me. I followed it. As if I had ceased to be a part of the world and found myself suspended in the emptiness between the earth and the escaping stars. I could only sense my body floating within that medium. I became a tight ball traveling to the unknown. Intensely, I searched the black for some explanation, some purpose for my confusion, but the billions of flickering fires only continued to swirl, transversing their path with obstinate fury.

In that moment of haze, the stars accelerated to flee my bewildered gaze. Orion abandoned his pursuit of Leo to find a new game to the southwest, Libra's scales tipped without balance, the serpent seethed and snapped its tail against the furious bear, and Polaris abandoned his northward destiny to follow the path of the long since fallen sun. Chaos reigned in this new reality; old standards subsided to need adventurous stars. The only feeling that I could fathom was that of the earth, no longer stationary but spinning beneath me at a speed of nearly one thousand miles per hour, and I was no longer in tandem with the orbiting spheres, but transcending that connection to occupy that limitless space around me. The stars beckoned with their deciphered code and that blackness invited my lost soul.

Yet as I flailed my arms to grasp hold of the fleeing granite, I was pulled back, out of the emptiness toward my seat at the edge of the point. The earth accepted me, caressed my head and offered me a place to seek refuge from the swirling chaos. So I accepted my haven there under the waving spruce branches beside the continuous flow of the ebbing tide, among the gulls and loons, amidst the muffled cries of the black ducks. No longer deluded, yet still feeling in confusion, I rested again, somewhat reluctantly, as the cold granite returned to its devious theft of my precious heat. The fireflies had dropped a net of nervousness over my befuddled form. I could not feign rejection of the hospitality of my host, my host who had sheltered me and offered me sustenance. I could only be grateful that in my desperation I had been received again. As the stars slowed and blackness came back into focus only a fleeting reminder of the wildness of space remained in the ephemeral flicker of a burning meteorite. I felt as if I had awoken from a dream into a dull reality. But the shock of the cold granite could not erase the memory of my journey, as the swirling stars, contrasted against the raging blackness, flashed through my mind.

Gravity sustained me. Unto the earth my body was delivered out of the chaos and order reappeared. The stars were muted once again as my understanding of space was limited to only my five senses and I was there not only inhabiting that spot, but existing with a purpose, for the earth had responded to my insecurity with outstretched arms. I now knew of my role, my essentiality. Gravity acknowledged my flight with a gesture that consoled me. Pulled out of my own confusion the salt spray tickled my face, and the moon cast a long shadow down to the base of the nearest red spruce. There on the granite, I was necessary. There, I could offer warmth; there I was part of a balance. Only there, the ceaseless interactions of man and nature continued, sustained my reality that someone would remember that wildness is endless.

We lived in cabins in the forest heated by wood stoves, which we maintained with wood we chopped earlier that week. There was a small sustainable farm where we all had chores to accomplish. There was always something to do. Plus, class work, which was harder that anything I had experienced. I was already doing college level course work. All of it made me more independent and stronger. A new appreciation for life grew and has stuck with me ever since.

There were two guy cabins and three girl cabins. After lights out we would sneak from cabin to cabin to play games and talk. There might have been a few sexual encounters but that was to be expected.

In January at four am, Zoe woke a bunch of us up and we ran into the mud of low tide. She ripped off her clothes and flew into the below freezing temperatures. She came out laughing and ran in again like it was the middle of summer and she was diving onto a Slip and Slide. Everyone dove in after her without hesitation. The mud was warming than the air and felt like a blanket over our goose bumped covered bodies. Of course, I bet I was the first one in after Zoe. Luckily for me, she was a full-blown lesbian. The first I had met my own age that was out of the closet and didn't shy away from it. She had no fear and it was magnetic. I immediately had very strong feelings for Zoe. She had black hair, blue eyes, and a smile that you always wanted to be around. To me she was undeniable. She quickly absorbed the outdoor Maine lifestyle despite having lived on the Upper West Side her whole life. She was wild, spontaneous, and always ready to soak up everything around her. I had never met anyone that was so courageous and ready to jump into all that is life.

But the rule at this school was no romance or sexual relationships of any kind because the group of us was so small it would cause conflict. The school focused on inclusiveness rather than exclusive relationships that were platonic or romantic. This was not to be accepted. They wanted us to all work together in harmony. We all thought that was a stupid rule, but it proved to be an important one to keep everyone connected and peaceful. Of course, though there was always flirting and sneaking out after lights out. No one could stop that. I went to visit her many times in New York City after the semester was over which was my first true lesbian experience beyond a kiss. It made me not want anything else. It was true and pure and passionate. It couldn't continue because of the distance, but from those moments on I began my search for that same feeling all over again.

Once she had come to Maine to visit and I told her that she could stay at my house. We would meet up with everyone else the next day and come home together. I had two waterbeds in my room. Some trashy movies might find that sexy or something but have you ever tried having sex on a waterbed? It's an awkward mess. We were both naked on our knees facing each other and I lost my balance and hit my chin on the edge of the wooden bed frame. Three of my teeth went completely through my bottom lip. There was blood everywhere. I had to have surgery for that too. I told my parents I had just lost my balance, which was surely very believable considering they found us before we could put on clothes because I was screaming so loudly. But I suppose everyone should have a dangerous sex story.

The people I met there changed me forever and even though I don't keep up with them anymore I hope they realize how much they have helped me. I hope somehow I made a difference in their lives as well. By the time I was finished, I knew the transition back home was going to be difficult. I now felt completely independent. I didn't need my parents for anything except love, which I could only get from my father. I had two jobs, I bought a car, and I was beginning my college applications. I didn't know how I was going to put up with this child / parent home life for another year.

I spent my senior year becoming closer to my father. He was always the strong silent type. Almost floating off into his own world. He had weird fears of unusual things. He had hardly any friends. Sometimes I would watch him tinkering with his truck in the driveway alone and he would be saying something and laughing. I thought, or rather hoped, maybe he was singing. He kept talking about how he knew Connie Chung from being in the Marines and that they had an affair. He would always say someday she will come back to me. He kept a picture of her in his sock drawer. Mom just said he was telling these stories just to make me laugh and they were simply based on fantasy. But there is a fine line between fantasy and delusion, which I was soon to completely understand. All these signs pointed out Schizophrenia in flashing lights.

A delusion is commonly defined as a fixed false belief and is used in everyday language to describe a belief that is either false, fanciful or derived from deception. Delusions typically occur in the context of neurological or mental illness, although they are not tied to any particular disease and have been found to occur in the context of many pathological states (both physical and mental). However, they are of particular diagnostic importance in psychotic disorders and particularly in schizophrenia.

A fantasy is a situation imagined by an individual or group, which does not correspond with reality but expresses certain desires or aims of its creator. Fantasies typically involve situations, which are impossible (such as the existence of magic powers) or highly unlikely (such as world peace). Fantasies can also be sexual in nature. In the theory of psychoanalysis, phantasy is used to describe unconscious desires, fears, drives etc. Sigmund Freud used the German word 'Phantasie', which could be translated as 'fantasy', but the meaning is clearly not the same as the everyday meaning and is usually printed as 'phantasy'. This should be strongly contrasted with delusion.

Dad was so gentle and careful and sensitive and kind. He taught me all I know about cars. He said that before I had my own car I had to know how to maintain it myself. My first car was a used black Mitsubishi Gallant. I loved it. I paid for half and my dad paid for the other half. That was the agreement. I am glad he had me put my money into it unlike all my wealthy friends that got their car hand pick from the dealer thanks to daddy's check. I paid the insurance, registration, and any inspection costs. The only other rule was that I had to learn how to change a tire, the oil, the spark plugs, the brake fluid, and jump-start the car. I loved those weekends when we would spend all afternoon covered in grease underneath the car. We were both such quiet people that only a few words were ever spoken, but it didn't feel quiet. It felt just right. It was a time without too much noise. I didn't know it then but it probably felt that way for him as well. We were so similar. With our hands and hard work this car became mine.

~ Seven ~

I ended up reconnecting with Carrie, friend of mine from the nearby town. Our mothers had been best friends for our whole lives and so being the same age we were like sisters. Unlike me, she had always been part of the cool crowd. The right clothes, the right eighties shaped bangs, and the expensive jeans. She even had the perfect white t-shirt to go underneath her coolest plaid flannel shirt and stonewashed jeans. You would think the mid-nineties would have had more style to offer, but you have to remember we were recovering from the eighties hip flare. But when it was just us there wasn't the hierarchy of high school crowds to invade our good time. Every year we would each visit each other's school for a couple days. Her life was so busy and focused on appearance and the right boyfriend and the right bangs. We liked spending time together so much that when we were little when one of our parents would come to take us home we could hide in the linen chest or the closet somehow thinking that they will let us be together just a little longer. Even though we grew up differently, we had so many young memories that kept us close when our lives began to move in separate directions, but this could only last for so long as I soon realized.

From a young age she was always dating various guys something I didn't really know about. She would tell me stories about what the penis looked like; apparently it had not been what she thought. "You know its not always hard, it can be soft and really tiny, not really appealing" or her most surprising discovery, "You know how there are two balls right? Well, that's not quite true, they are both in the same sack. You can feel two of them but it just looks kind if like one!" She said that that guys shouted out with pleasure when you squeezed one of their balls real hard. I had to break it too her that this probably wasn't pleasure, but intense pain. Maybe I hadn't seen it with my own eyes but I think I had it all more figured out than she did.

The summer before my senior year of high school her friends were having a big end of summer party and she invited me to come. I hadn't seen her in a while, but catching up had always been something we were good at in the past. I knew most of her friends over the years from parties for this or that. As with any high school bash, there were plenty of alcohol, pills, and other recreational goods. At the time I was very straight, clean, and uptight about all that, so I put some juice in one of those plastic red party cups and sipped it slowly through the night. There was this one guy Matt who I used to go to the beach together with when we were little. I could tell he liked me. Not just because of the alcohol either, but his body language made it pretty darn obvious. Maybe I could try and like him? Maybe, not. I liked the idea of him liking me, but I couldn't get past his Adams apple and overgrown sideburns. I enjoyed talking to him. He was easy going, and non-threatening.

At some point, I had to pee and quickly found Carrie to hold my drink while I went. I didn't want to just leave it somewhere with someone I didn't know. I had watched too many of those Dateline specials about the date rape drug. When I came back I took my lemonade from Carrie and continued talking to Matt. Within fifteen minutes I blacked out. Many hours later we both woke up naked in someone's bedroom. In a panic, I immediately stood up; sheets wrapped around me, and began yelling at him. What I said at the moment is a bit of a blur but it certainly involved accusing him of taking advantage of me, and being an asshole. That he just wanted to fuck a virgin. He sat there listening while I went on and on until I took a breath and he started asking me the same questions I had been asking him. The same accusations.

When we both calmed down a bit we realized that we both had been slipped something in our drinks. At that point I called Carrie and asked her if she knew what had happened. She laughed and laughed. I remember the cruel cackle in her throat. She was so glad her practical joke had worked. She had drugged both of us. I was so fucking pissed. What type of friend is she? How could this have even happened? I thought we had been friends our whole lives. I was never to speak with her again. After Matt and I dealt with our anger, we actually ended up developing a good friendship. He introduced me to a female friend of his, and well, let's just say that worked out well for a while too in many ways.

Have you seen the show "Hoarders" or ever heard of a hoarder"? It isn't about people that are just messy or lazy. It is a mental disorder that causes you to keep things even if they are worthless, hazardous, or unsanitary. One of my aunts was such a woman. During the middle of my summer vacation, my mother decided that we were going to clean her basement for her. Every piece of soiled trash we would try to throw out she would find some excuse to keep it. There was anything that I would rather be doing, but parted me wanted to help out this poor woman. He life had completely spiraled out of control. And after all, who else was going to take them time to help her. My aunt and her children were in a dangerous situation. The basement was covered head to toe in feces. And it was full about six feet high of junk. We spent three days trashing, emptying and then washing everything with bleach. There were no windows and just a narrow stairway out. At some point the concentration of bleach was so strong I had to run outside to catch my breath. I felt like I had been contaminated.

Right after my mother and I cleaned up the best we could we

went canoeing on the Saco River overnight and then went home. The next morning I woke up and I couldn't move. I had the worse pain in my head and neck I think anyone could possibly have. I couldn't sit up. I felt like I was going to pass out. I needed help. I yelled as loudly as I could which wasn't as loud as it should have been and eventually my father found me. He said my mother was having the same symptoms. He carried me into the car. I was worse off than my mother who actually walked to the car. The second we arrived at the hospital the nurses took one look at us and rushed us into the isolation room.

Everyone that came in was in full white protective outfits. They did a quick spinal tap and determined we both had advanced bacterial meningitis. Mine was worse because I was only sixteen. They brought my dad in the room in a white suit to tell me that I had four hours to live because they couldn't reverse it. They weren't quite sure how long my mother had yet. I was on so many drugs but I was still in so much pain that I was actually relieved when I heard I had four hours left. I couldn't stand this any longer than that. I was sure this would be my end. I just knew it. I was so happy my father was not sick. They weren't sure what caused it. Was it the cleaning? The river? Or just chance? I was toxic and slipping under.

But four hours passed and I was still breathing. Somehow I had made it passed their expectations. I probably should have been happy but I asked them to give me enough pain medicine to kill me. I couldn't take it anymore. I don't know if I can possibly express how severe and terrifying the pain was. Plus, everyone we saw was in full protective gear. I felt like I was an alien or something. Eventually, they moved us into a more long-term isolation unit together. We were there for six weeks.

When we were discharged, we remained on pain medicine for quite some time. My senior year was approaching and I didn't know how I was even going to do the normal school work let alone the outward-bound adventure they had planned for us. The school had separated us into groups of nine and we had to hike the Appalachian Trail for two weeks before school started as some kind of bonding experience. I hadn't even considered going. I knew I couldn't do it. I just had been sick for over a month with a near deadly illness. I was weak and still had rebound head pain.

But then my mother bought me an expensive hiking backpack and everything I would need to go along with it. What was she thinking? I mean how could I not take this moment in my life to hike along the Appalachian trail. Sure, it made perfect sense. How sympathetic of her. I told her to take it back. She threatened me and said if I gave her any resistance that she would tell the Headmaster that I was lying about my illness. What the fuck was she thinking? She told the school that I was healthy and I was making up the whole meningitis thing. With a lot of force, I went.

I was exhausted, hyperventilating, and could barely carry my bag. At first they had the strongest leader carry my bag for me and I remained at the end of the line. That was not even enough. I never should have gone. At one point I passed out. The trees started blurring and spinning around me and then I lost feeling in my legs. After that, the next thing I remember was being strapped to the Spine Board. I was scared because my vision was so grey and I had no idea what was going on. So many people were all yelling at once. "Sara, Sara, SARA!" They kept repeatedly yelling my name with no question. What did they want me to do or say? I was in shock, which is caused by an insufficient blood flow throughout the body. This can cause many other injury and illnesses. They were worried that I might suffer from a heart attack because there wasn't enough oxygen in my body's tissues. Luckily, help got there just in time to prevent my symptoms from worsening rapidly. They brought me to the nearest hospital. Child Protective Services investigated my mother for child endangerment. She claimed stupidity and nothing came of it, but I had hoped it taught her something. It didn't. It taught her another way she could control my life and the situation that I lived in. Slowly, in her sick mind she was becoming God.

After surviving death combined with the confidence I had gained from my semester away led to a touch of arrogance. The beginning of that school year I thought I had it all under control; an obnoxious error for anyone to make. I had new clothes, new hair, and most of all a new attitude. I had *NSYNC and Mariah Carey blasting on my car radio. I felt like I could accomplish anything. My mother tried to take credit for my newfound confidence.

"You are what you are because of me, you know."

"No, I am what I am despite you."

I had only been gone one semester from my old school. Even though I made an effort to write letters and make phone calls when they were allowed, all my old friends thought that I had abandoned them. They thought that I didn't care and now I would rather be with my new friends but this wasn't the case. I still cared about them deeply. Now I believe that if they had been more mature they would have been happy for me. And maybe if I had been I would have understood where they were coming from. Things eventually changed back, but it wasn't the welcome home I had anticipated.

Thinking about coming out to my friends and family had been running through my mind for quite some time. Living away from home and being in a place where I could live my true feelings proudly and happily pushed me towards opening up and telling my little secret. Now that I was stronger I was beginning to realize that if someone was not going to accept me for such a personal choice they didn't need to be in my life. I was willing to take that risky step thanks to growing self-esteem and self-assurance. It wasn't up to me to change what anyone believed. All I could do was focus on myself to stay strong and balanced if I was going to be successful with my life.

I didn't come out to my parents until I started secretly dating a friend of mine halfway through senior year. Mother insisted that it was a phase. That I was trying to be cool, hang out with a different crowd. Who ever wanted to be gay because it was cool? She accused me of lying to her all of these years. I wasn't lying. I was trying to make things work out so I could be "normal". She made me feel guilty for not telling her sooner. As if I had known all this time that she would be cool with it. She blamed me for telling her that something that was just a phase was going to be my reality. I realized that gay or straight it didn't matter with her. She would find someway to find me at fault during such a vunerable time so she could manipulate me through guilt, regret, and shame. I told her when it felt like there was no turning back. This was not a phase.

"You are directly from the devil"; a quote my Baptist great grandmother would use to affectionately describe me. It was still illegal at that time. Why would you ever want that for yourself? There was no hope to ever get married. Dad just told me to be careful. He said he wanted me to be happy, but with so many ignorant people out there he said keep it a secret, don't flaunt it. Sometimes being overly confident turns into ignorance. I remember these words very specifically, "They'll kill you, Sara, they will." He wasn't ashamed or disappointed. He just seemed sad and worried about the life that I would be forced to live. And he gave me a long hug.

I had started to fall in love with a good friend of mine, Eva. She had blond curly hair and a curvy figure to die for. She was smart, very funny and wanted to eventually be a stand up comedian. At first, she was sincere and excited. So much energy. We began spending all of our time together. It felt like we could never get sick of each other. We could talk all day on end. About what? Anything.

But even from the beginning, I knew it probably wouldn't last. We both had applied to separate colleges before we started dating and neither one of us made the decision to change that. Maybe we were both scared. She had never been with a girl before or even had seen herself being with one, but I could tell immediately she liked me. In the first flush everything seemed perfect; laughing, understanding, supportiveness, and great sex. I always felt like somehow I had led her into the dark world of homosexuality. She would enjoy people staring at us, especially guys. I was only looking at her. It bothered me a little when I felt like she liked being the focus of some kind of show; the focus of affection. I didn't care what anyone thought at first. We were happy and naïve.

The last year of high school was completely centered on college applications because Waynflete was not going to have someone not get into a four-year college after graduation. I hadn't really thought about college before they started drilling me about who I was and what did I want to be. I had just figured that there was no money for college so I better forget about it. I knew I could be successful without a college degree. I mean these schools they were suggesting that I apply to were upwards of forty thousand dollars for just one year. But everyone didn't see money as an issue because of my grades, SAT scores, and extracurricular activities.

What I didn't know was that my grandma had spent her whole life setting aside a nest egg for me to have the best college experience money could buy. She said she would pay anything my scholarships didn't cover. She didn't want me to have any loans after college. This is one of the best gifts she could have ever have given me. Her dream of being an educated woman would now be my reality.

Waynflete demanded that each student apply to seven colleges by the fall deadline. It was a plan to make sure you would get in somewhere. Applying to a few reach schools, some middle ground, and of course two safety schools. Safety schools were ones that couldn't possibly reject you.

It all happened so fast that I didn't even feel like there was time for me to say, "No, this isn't what I want". Someone somewhere along the line I decided should study pre-med at a liberal arts school with a child psychology major. Or did this get decided for me? The good thing though is that I didn't have any worries. I began to realize that I was a solid candidate. I had a perfect GPA, 1550 on my SAT score (that's with the old way of counting), plus I was a professional dancer, a female pilot and I played the violin. But the thing about college you can have perfect coming out of your ass and they will still reject you. So like they told me, I applied to seven schools. I got into all but one; Tufts. But that is okay. I had to really look closely and think about what I wanted so I narrowed it down to two schools and visited them both before deciding.

I first went to Swarthmore. Surely it is the more prestigious of the schools. It was intimidating. There is this overwhelming silence. But it wasn't just the architecture that was cold it was the people too. I hardly saw anyone outside. All everyone talked about was how much studying they did and never really mentioned anything that they did for fun. Sure, it is one of the top schools in the country, but would I enjoy myself? Could I really live here for four years? Plus they were only giving me a partial scholarship.

During the time when I was getting my acceptance letters, a wooden crate came in the mail. Inside was five pounds of Walla Walla Sweet Onions to say congratulations for getting in to Whitman College. It was definitely the most original way of saying welcome. Walla Walla Sweet Onions are known all over the country. Just go to your grocer and one of the piles of onions will say Walla Walla Sweets. I don't even like onions but these you can eat just like an apple they are that good. So next I flew all the way out to Walla

Walla, Washington to try and see if Whitman was going to be the school of my dreams.

I went in the beginning of spring, which I later learned is the most beautiful time of the year to visit. It is this little paradise on the southeastern corner of the state surrounded by a mountain range, which protects it from all the rain, that Seattle and the rest of the state is known for. It is about seventy-five degrees and sunny from March until October every year and no harsh winters. At that time the town was mostly Mexican. All the signs, menus, prices, bathrooms were in Spanish. It was a great opportunity to meet some amazing people and sharpen my Spanish speaking skills. Whitman was a little sanctuary away from the onion and taco truck wasteland that surrounded us. It was like being in a totally different place. The town and the college felt divided. There was always a lot of unnecessary tension between the town and the school, which was unfortunate for everyone involved. But at the time when I was visiting, it didn't effect my decision.

From the moment I arrived it felt right. I slept over one night to see how I liked it and the students couldn't have been nicer. I had a meeting with the Director of Admissions, which I spent two days preparing for by trying to think of what answers to say and what not to say. What questions should I ask to give the right impression? I wanted him to know all I had done in my short life without looking like I was bragging. Should I try and lose my Maine accent? But he just brought me in and told me all the reasons why they picked me and that I would have a full scholarship. I didn't have to sell myself, he was selling me the college. I would just have to pay for food and board. I was blown away. Someone actually wanted me to attend their college? It gave me so much confidence to use for the upcoming years. It was the place I had really been looking for and I could care less if no one in Maine knew about it. To me it was a hidden gem.

So I made my decision and the rest of the school year flew by. For my high school graduation, we didn't wear gowns. Girls had to be in white dresses and guys were to be in black suits. It gave a more formal feeling to the event rather than putting on some black moo moo. We didn't even have graduation caps. It was an intimate celebration because of how small our class was. Two of the more alternative guys didn't even come. They said they were against it and they would get their diploma whether they were there or not. All the girls decided to take off their shoes at some point. We didn't want to risk tripping. So as each of us rose to get out diploma we walked barefoot. I didn't see the problem, but my grandfather never stopped talking about that for the rest of his life. What a disgrace he would say, how could you bring down the celebration like that when you are supposed to be fine-bred women? He wasn't overly serious and eventually years later we had a laugh over it.

~ Eight ~

Academics have always been effortless for me. Once I read something I can recall the image and the information on it relatively quickly. At one point it could be said I had a photographic memory, but with the progression of my disease and collective trauma my skills have lessened. Even though it is easier for me to read pages upside down, it never prevented me from doing well in school. But now was the true test. It was time to head of to college. It may have appeared like I was strong and happy but through this transition it felt like my world fell apart. No, I didn't just feel it. My life really did collapse.

At night, I lived in constant paralyzing fear. I didn't want to talk about it with anyone. Some would say I was isolated, nonsocial, wanting to be alone, but that wasn't really it. My mind was so occupied with conversations I felt like I was around too many people all the time already. How could I really truly concentrate on what someone else was talking about? Do you know how hard it is to separate four conversations at once, especially when three of them are in your head. How was I going to be able to appropriately reply? How was I supposed to tell what was real? I had so much anxiety sometimes I felt like I was going to implode. I mean literally crush in on myself. I tried to keep my breathing regular, but that only takes you so far. It doesn't quiet your mind. And for those who tell me to meditate, well, I'm sorry. You can try meditating with Larry and Maggie when you want. Go right ahead, enjoy, but don't include me.

How am I supposed to quiet my mind when my mind is what is broken in the first place? First I would hear them giggling from the other part of my room. In the beginning stages, before Larry and

Maggie, there were usually three girls. Completely unrelated to my temporary sisters from the past or anyone else I had ever known. Their silhouettes would dance on the ceiling and around my bed. They would tell me that I should never have been the one to survive. It was time to say goodbye to this world because they weren't going to stop. They would just get more persistent.

At this time I began cutting myself with razor blades to try to stop feeling the emotional pain. I just wanted the voices to stop. In fact, that is all I have ever wanted. Just like with any addiction I had a routine to go with it. I would always use a new razor each time; take off the cardboard wrapping, taste the metallic flavor of the blade, and place cotton balls beside me. It was a compulsion to control the fear I had from my emotions spiraling out of control. I didn't do it for attention as some might. I didn't want anyone to know. Ever. So I would cut. First it was my lower arms, but then I had to start wearing long sleeved shirts so no one would find out. So then I started cutting my upper thighs so I could at least wear short-sleeved shirts. But by then it had gone so far that I had to drop out of swimming class. Make up only covers so much.

After you go through with it, after you cut, there is an immediate sense of relief as if all the bad emotions you were having had just poured out of you, and then you fall to the floor with guilt. The shift is very sudden. Why did I do this? What if someone finds out? I don't want them to worry or to know. I didn't want this to be someone else's problem. And I didn't want to be this person that would cut up her body. How could I be so weak? Or maybe the question is how could I let the voices become so controlling? It got to a point where I would do most anything they told me to avoid hearing them. To try and just make them shut the fuck up. It took a long time for me to realize that and even now I find myself sometimes succumbing to their words.

Whitman College required that you live on campus your first two years to keep everyone integrated and social. By chance, my first roommate was Andi. She wasn't exactly beautiful, but her long blond hair, big boobs, and easiness was an automatic attraction for most guys. In the beginning, it seemed like we got along fantastically. I was not attracted to her at all and she seemed like she could be a good friend. We would even shut the door to keep everyone out so we could spend time talking alone, just us. At first, the only problem was that she brought home a different guy every weekend (sometimes two) and sleep with them in my room. So I would be forced to go sleep on the couches in the common area of the residential hall.

Despite this, she was my closest friend at school in the very beginning. I even told her I was dating a girl long distance but she didn't seem to care. Well, at least then.

I got close with several girls and guys in my residential hall. Especially, Kate and Terra who lived right next to me. I was a roommate with both of them over the years. They were wonderful friends in very different ways. Terra is more serious and abstract and Kate is more balanced and silly. They had all skipped a grade and were a year too young just like me. It was an interesting coincidence. The two of them are such smart, fun, and creative individuals who were always there for me through all the ups and downs of my college experience.

Eva and I talked on the phone obsessively each night. I thought we were committed to each other. But later I was to find out that she had already found someone else to sleep with just one month into our long distance relationship. I had no idea until right before we broke up. I was devastated. She had always put so much control on me from the start. Be home at this time, who are you going with, where will you be, what will I be doing. She was about one thousand miles away. It felt like she was obsessed with controlling my every move. If I wanted to be with my new friends in college or even had to study she would usually hang up the phone on me. This part got worse and worse. Over half the time she would call me just to say that we were breaking up or were on a break. The rollercoaster stress was impossible to take. So I suggested that we try and move closer together. I thought it would fix everything. So we talked and decided she would apply to my school and I would hers and whoever got in would transfer so we could be together. She said she applied, but I could tell she didn't want to switch schools for me. I never saw any applications or letters of rejection. She just told me they wouldn't take her. So even though I got in to her school, I lied. I said I didn't get in. I regretted that I had suggested moving in the first place. I didn't want to move over one thousand miles to be with someone who didn't love me. How embarrassing. Truth is we were both playing games.

Immediately there became a issue between the two of us. Since she had grown up in a traditional paternal family. She told me that for our relationship to work she was to be the girl and I would be the guy. I had to do everything to support her and keep her safe no matter what. She never considered reciprocating. That was not an option. But I was not a man. I knew I never would be one even if I occasionally acted a little like a tomboy or wore less feminine clothes. I think because she wanted to imagine I was a man and it made her not want to touch me sexually. She wanted to deny that part of me. She just stopped touching me. Everything was one sided and I was to always keep my clothes on. This problem got worse and worse over the years. Eventually she told me that she felt like going down on me was disgusting and just feeling my wet vaginal made her skin feel like it was crawling. I felt like I must be disgusting. Her comments penetrated most of my thoughts. Just what every woman wants to hear. It made me to begin to feel asexual. It wasn't until I finally left her years later I realized that I did deserve to be loved and desired just like my partner. This brought back my feminine side that I had lost a connection with. Luckily, I am far from that now.

When Thanksgiving break was coming I knew that it was too short of a time to fly home so Andi invited me to stay with her family in Salem, Oregon just south of Portland. It sounded like fun and I couldn't wait to meet the rest of her family. I went to her house and at first everyone seemed so kind and curious about Andi's new best friend. One evening when we were sitting for dinner her parents asked about out love lives. Before Andi said anything about herself she exclaimed, "Sara is in a long distance relationship with a girl." It felt like a spotted elephant fell on the table. When they asked her about herself she pushed the conversation towards my little secret.

That night after I had supposedly gone to bed I overheard whispering in the kitchen. I snuck like a pancake against the side of the wall and listened. What I heard went something like this, "Andi, you can't share a room with a lesbian. What if she is looking at you the wrong way and then she attacks you?" Her dad agreed, "You can no longer socialize with this, this, thing, this pervert." "And definitely don't change in front of her. She is a predator." How could she just take her parents word for it? How ignorant was she? The words crawled up my spine and almost chocked me. What was I to do? Hitchhike back to Walla Walla in the middle of the night? My heart was racing. I was trapped. I knew she would continue to be my roommate for the rest of the year. I could have complained to the Dean, and maybe, been able to move away from her, but I wasn't confident enough yet. We drove in silence for the whole four hours back to school.

And it was tough. I went from being her best friend to her enemy just because what her parents had said. From the moment we arrived back on campus she never talked to me again. It happened that fast. I had been switched off. She acted like I had never even existed. She wouldn't even change a sweatshirt in front of me. She told every girl on the unit that I was out to get them. That all I wanted was their bodies. We had communal shower for our section to use. I noticed every girl would never change in there anymore. It was so uncomfortable. At that point, I would have given anything to be straight just like everyone else. Pretty soon I started using the guys bathroom upstairs. I didn't know what else to do. At least they didn't mind.

Before all this had happened, Andi, Terra, and myself had applied to live in the only three-person room in the building. We even had our separate bathroom than the rest of the hall. At first it seemed like a dream, but after my blowout with Andi I knew it would be a mess. Especially since Terra was bisexual herself and I had grown very close to her as a friend. In addition, Terra would have these huge swings in mood that I didn't know about until we moved in together. I would come home and I never knew what I was walking into. Now, that I can look back at it all I think she was suffering from bipolar disorder or maybe just trauma over losing her father. Andi became a full bitch. She took over the main area forcing the two of us to sleep in the space of a closet. And even though we had a bathroom she had to walk through our space to get there so she never used it. How come gay means pervert anyhow?

Luckily, there was Julia. I called her Jules. She wasn't a student of the college. I met her because she would come from Portland, Oregon to visit her college friends. She was half Indian, half Native American. Ignorant people would call her the double Indian behind her back. The second I was introduced to her at a party I wanted her. I had laser focus. I had never felt such a strong physical attraction before. And she was the same with me. I loved to take pictures of her. She was my muse. She had her separate life and I had mine, but when we were together it felt like nothing else existed. We had no rules, limitations, or monogamy. We just enjoyed our monthly visit together and it was free and easy. Our time together was always limited and therefore much more intense. Since Eva and I were pretty much always on some kind of break I never felt like I was cheating on her. You can interpret it how you will, but I was just trying to be happy.

With Eva I felt like I was always leading her into the world of lesbianism. But with Jules, we both in it and it was always on. She made me even more confident about my own identity. When we were around each other we couldn't keep our hands off each other. We couldn't help ourselves. So maybe it wasn't right, but when my girlfriend would yell and say she never wanted to talk to me there was Jules. I never said I was perfect.. After I graduated from college I never saw Jules again. She was a shimmering mirage trapped in time lifting me out of the darkness I was burying myself in.

But then just before winter break Terra's father died. He had been suffering from early onset Alzheimer's for many years. His brain finally forgot how to do automatic functions like breathing or making your heartbeat. I was with her when she got the call in the hallway. She just collapsed and hit the floor. Even though she knew that his death was approaching it didn't make it any easier. She seemed like she was in shock before she was able to get an early plane ride home. She became so shut off from everyone, including me, that I worried deeply about her. I hoped that going home would give her some kind of resolution.

The following March, just three months later, my father either killed himself or my mother shot him. You would think it should be clear right? I think the amount of grief that Terra and I had brought us closer together. We could talk about anything together for hours at a time. We were so close in many ways. Our hugs and kisses over the years always felt like friendship and respect but not necessarily sexual. We felt like that the only person who would understand us were each other. I didn't realize it at the time but a delusion of mine drove us apart. Now I am here in Maine and I have

no freaking clue where she is or even if she would talk to me.

~ Nine ~

Here is a murder mystery of sorts. Not a delusion or hallucination but rather reality. What actually happened cannot quickly be decided but rather you must mull it over. I believe the truth reveals itself. My first year of college, I was coming home from Washington State back to Maine for my two-week spring break. Blizzards were just one after another. The biggest one of the season stopped me from making it home in time. We tried to fly into Portland and made it all the way to the runway but couldn't land so we had to turn back to Detroit.

During my layover in Detroit, I got a phone call from my mother, "Dad has been acting odd. His speech has been slurring and he seems very distant." This information didn't worry me too much since Dad had been struggling with schizophrenia during his whole life. But I figured the warning from my mother must mean something so I was alert from the moment I saw him. As much as I could see he was just a little quieter than normal. He actually warned me that my mother was acting weird, out of control, and her lying, which had always been a problem, increased ten fold. I was certain this was not a delusion. My mothers own insane behavior was most certainty believable. Somehow it felt normal to me. Maybe now that I was no longer living at home the gloves were off.

Dad always had an immense sense of fear of doctors and hospitals but my mother insisted on taking him to the emergency room. On the way, he jumped out of the car while she was driving on four lane road that led to the hospital. I felt like she was just trying to torture him. His dead weight hit hard. Luckily, cars were able to swerve out of the way in time. After the fall, he was disorientated enough that we were able to get him back into the car. Eventually, we arrived and, surprise, the doctors found no problems. He came back home.

He took some time off work and went back the following Monday. He wanted to go back and seemed in a better mood. While he was at work my mother showed me these childlike drawings that my father had supposedly done with crayon. My father never drew a day in his life and they looked like something my mother came up with. I tried to just brush aside her lie so she wouldn't get anything out of it. She was full of lies and manipulations. In fact, she was a master of it. It was almost to the point of having to separate her from my life.

Since coming home, I had been staying with friends. Plus, Eva and I had temporarily patched things up. I told my parents that because my break overlapped with my friends during the first week that I would spend the first week with them and the second with my parents. That particular night – that Monday – was the first night I stayed home. As usual, Dad cooked dinner and put the leftovers in the fridge. In fact, he even said we could all eat them together tomorrow.

I watched some of his favorite shows with him while my

mother was busy doing I don't know what. Probably eating an entire bag of Hershey Kisses or playing with her paperwork. She would make an enormous aluminum foil ball from the kisses with each bag she inhaled. The sound of her heavy breathing as she inhaled the chocolate drove me crazy. Eventually, it was time for me to go up to my room and read for a bit before bed. As I was heading up the stairs he said, "I'll see you in the morning. I love you. " I said the same back thought nothing of it. It was what we always said. I read for a bit and then went on my computer chatting with Eva. There was a giant blizzard that night and large limbs kept falling on the skylights from the weight of the snow. It was very noisy. I had trouble falling asleep.

It was 2:20am and I was still messaging on my laptop to Eva. And then I heard the loudest noise of my life. It was nothing like the movies. The type of noise was one that I had never heard before. It felt like it was coming from right below me, which was my parent's bedroom. I ran downstairs. My mother was awake on the couch watching crap on the TV. She was sitting straight up instead of lying down. Even in the moment it struck me as odd. Panicking, I just kept demanding an answer from my mother, "Didn't you hear that noise, what was it? You heard it. I know you head it. What was that noise?" I was frantic and stammering. She said maybe it was a snow-covered branch falling on a skylight. This didn't seem believable for a second.

She seemed relaxed as I ran around the house with my head cut off. I ran down the basement and couldn't find the source of the noise and then it hit me, "Why didn't dad hear the noise? Why isn't he up?" I kept demanding an answer from my mother. I ran down the hall to their bedroom and the door was closed. As I grabbed for the door knob my mother screamed while running down the hallway to catch up behind me, "Don't open the door. Sara, don't." I didn't hesitate. I opened it anyway and saw what no one should ever see: my naked father with a gunshot through his face.

The air got sucked out of the room. My mother didn't seem to have much of a reaction except for saying I never should have pushed opened the door. But why would she say that if she really, truly, didn't know what was behind that door? Her telling me, "Don't open the door," to me, screams guilty. Doesn't it? But I didn't have time to process every moment until later. My immediate reaction was to run, get the phone, and call for help. I still had the internet hooked up to the phone line. I ran up to my room and pulled the cord out of the wall and grabbed the phone laying in my bed. Deep in my heart I knew it was too late but I didn't know what else too do. The whole house smelt like gunpowder. A smell I had never encountered in my life and hope to never again. The bitterness still gags me.

I dialed 911 and spoke with them from the living room. My mother wasn't with me, but I wasn't thinking about that. I was just trying to get help. The operator made me stay on the phone until the police got there. I don't remember what was said. What I didn't realize until the police questioned me later was that when I went to get the phone and called the police my mother entered the bedroom to supposedly see if he was alive. She insisted she didn't touch anything. But according to the police her fingerprints were all over the gun. But the prints were not enough. After all, this was her home too so why wouldn't her finger prints already be everywhere. But the thing is, that gun was kept high on the wall in the back of the garage covered in spider webs all the years I lived there. Her finger prints wouldn't have just been there. The investigators said he was shot at an abnormal angle for a suicide, but couldn't prove that she had done it herself even with all my testimony and evidence.

I remember just sitting on the white kitchen tiles trying to put it all together while medics and police flooded in and out the creaky screen door. But I couldn't put my thoughts together. I was no longer able to. Shock was settling in. My body just couldn't handle this much information. I didn't even want to. Even at that moment I knew I would remember the exact temperature of the floor on my toes forever. I didn't want to think my mother had killed him. But it didn't quite make sense that he had done it himself either. The police never charged her with murder.

My grandfathers obsession with police scanners ended that night after he heard, "Fatal gunshot wound at forty seven Old Blue Point Road. Most likely suicide. All back up required." Not what anyone ever should have to hear about their son. He told me that the second he heard it he knew it was about my dad. About an hour later, when the emergency crews were leaving he came to take me home to his house. He told my mother she had out figure out another place to stay. That was when I realized he suspected that she was involved in this. When he came to get me from the police station he attempted to ignore my mother, but she kept getting in his face. He said firmly, "I know you had a heavy hand in all of this, Pam Please stay away". I went back to his house. It was starting to get light out by then, but I climbed into bed beside him. He held me tight.

And even today twelve years later, I am not sure what to believe but more and more because of the events which followed his death I can't stop thinking that she got away with murder. After all, she got a half a million dollar insurance policy that she swore up and down she never recieved because he committed suicide. But my lawyers several years later proved that she got the full amount seven days after he passed away fooling everyone to think that he screwed us over and that she as broke when she was floating in cash.

At a time when I was in shock and barely talking, my mother thought it was best that I go back to college as soon as possible. She made up some bullshit that the quicker I went back to school the quicker I would get back to normal. No one agreed with her including doctors, friends, and family. But I didn't want to be around her either so I went with it. She also told me that there would be a lot of financial problems she must deal with since he passed away. With me going back to college she asked me to sign a financial power of attorney so she could take care of the necessary tasks, which I didn't think would amount to much, while I was far away. Unfortunately, in a moment of weakness I believed my mother and signed the documents.

But this was the worst mistake of my life. Why did I do it? Why would I have trusted her after all that? At that moment, the situation wasn't as clear as it looks now. I didn't want to be alone. I didn't want her to be so horrible. I wanted to believe that she wouldn't go so far. I had just lost my father. I needed to believe in something good, I guess. And I think part of me just wanted to be done with the whole situation, to sign it over and be done with it.. How was I supposed to know what would happen? I was in a completely vulnerable state which my mother used to attach to me like a leech.

I remember showing back at college two weeks later than everyone else. My close friends knew what had really happened. I had called to tell them previously why I wouldn't be there on time so they wouldn't worry. The night I arrived I told Kate and Terra the story. As I try to recall how I told it or even their reactions I can't remember. It is more than just a blur; it is gone along with the next month or so. All I know is that for the next four months I would jolt myself awake at exactly 2:20am every morning. Time had made an imprint on my soul.

After I went back to school, my mother made attempts to make my friends believe that I was out to harm them. There was also many phone calls to the Dean of Students that quickly led to him getting a restraining order against my mother. Everyone was trying to take me away from her clammy grasp. She needed to own me. Luckily, my school didn't believe the lies and they helped me to separate myself from my mother but unfortunately I did lose friends during several incidents.

~Ten ~

I went into college so sure of myself. The plan was to be a child psychiatrist. I would take all the credits necessary to be pre-med and major in psychology at the same time. But as soon as I took my first art class I was hooked. I loved the classes and I even loved the homework. I just couldn't stop creating. It became the coping skill I needed to help me get through what felt like was the hardest part of my life.

My first professor was named David Wharton who I consider one of the best watercolorist in the country. He taught me control. We spent the first month learning to draw perfectly straight lines with a brush without any tracing. He always said you only need one medium sized brush and if you know how to use it you can do anything. While holding the brush he would put an egg in the palm of our hands. You needed to keep your hand open, hold onto the egg with the muscles in the palm of your hand and control the brush with your fingers. Remain in control and don't allow your hand to touch the paper. At first it was such a challenge. He bought me my first nice brush.

This semester went so well that I started taking oil painting and drawing classes with the head of the department, Keiko Hara. Originally from Japan, she had a very strong accent despite living and attending three colleges in the United States the past forty years. She was so round with tiny little legs. She reminded me of a young girl in a peach Halloween costume. She is an internationally infamous painter and has several galleries. Her work is even at the National Printmaking Museum. She was the toughest teacher I had ever had.

We would work on these paintings she called "progress

paintings" that were six by four foot sheets of heavy duty paper. The paper could handle a lot of work. Every semester we did one. They could be painting, drawing, collage, anything that inspired you and your original theme. We had to come up with some sort of theme and paint and repaint the same piece over and over drastically changing it without changing the theme every week. You couldn't just cover up what you had before and paint something totally new. The painting had to have a connection to its past and a leap towards it's future. If you only changed a couple colors she would tear it in half. I think she thought we were wasting her time. We all became so invested in these paintings. Over four months had been spent working and reworking them for at least three to four hours a day outside of class. And that was just for one class, I was taking four others at the same time.

And then one day, she told us to put our paintings on the floor. She had trays with gesso in them. Gesso, if you are not a painter, is a hard compound of plaster that you put on your canvas as a base prior to painting. Basically, it is thick white paint that covers everything. Next we were made to take off our shoes and socks. She made us step in the gesso and then walking all over our paintings, our hard work. Some people tried to just take a few careful steps, which resulted in her pouring the gesso container all over the paper. We were all pissed. How could she do this to us? Hadn't she seen how hard we worked? But that was exactly the point. She wanted us to recognize the impermanence of our creations. That we could rebuild and it would be a thousand times better because of the lesson we learned. Rebuilding led to progress, creativity, and imagination.

David and I became very close. Just within walking distance, I went to his house several times a week. There was no physical attraction, but mentally I just couldn't get enough. He had a full photography studio in his home where we took pictures of my artwork and made new exciting pieces. He introduced me to digital arts and how to combine them with traditional media. In 2000, this was a new concept with the launch of the first digital cameras. I quickly got one of the first five-megapixel Nikon cameras ever made. Because of my focus in this area, I wrote a grant to Apple and Epson to help me build a digital media studio at my school. They gave me five computers, three printers, and a lifetime supply of ink. One of the printers was four foot wide so you could put anything through it. Canvas, homemade paper, clothing, whatever you wanted. I immediately became the founder and creator of the first digital media lab at Whitman College. It paid well and I loved it.

Sadly, David was going through a very difficult time. He had lost his wife, daughter, and booming business in Sun Valley, Idaho. He enjoyed teaching but it just wasn't enough for him. He got drunk every night, which in turn just made him more depressed. I went to his house almost every night just to say hi and check in. But just checking in rapidly became me obsessively watching over him. I found him at the kitchen table with a loaded gun in his right hand with the safety off.

I stood here frozen. Time moved slowly. How could this be happening to someone else in my life? Again, come on? I pleaded with him to just give me the gun. I said that I would spend the night at his house so he wasn't lonely and how much he was loved by so many. I was stuttering. I was more than nervous. He put the gun right up to his temple. I flew at him and grabbed the gun. He was a little slow because of the alcohol. It went off sending the bullet flying into the kitchen wall. I took the ammunition out and threw it outside, poured some lighter fluid on top, and set it ablaze. I was desperate. I I couldn't do anything to stop his depression, at least I stopped his plan for the rest of the night. had to save him. But I felt my body clench. What was this feeling? And then I realized that I was pissed. I was actually angry at him. How could he have done this to me?

From then on I always felt like it was my responsibility, my duty, to help him through his life. But was all my help useless? Was I useless? I would get so frustrated. I didn't know what I would do if I lost him too. I knew that I would feel like it was all my fault no matter the circumstances. I wanted to help him the best I knew how, but does anyone really know what that is. It felt like because I couldn't save my father, I had to help him. Anytime he got too drunk or too depressed, I was there at his doorstep watching over him like a small child. He was a responsibility that I was not equipped to deal with and shouldn't of felt like I had to be.

Instinctually, I introduced Terra to him and immediately there was a spark. They started dating right away. He was actually starting to smile. When he had doubts I would start lecturing about how happy they were. I was gong to make this work. They each filled a hole in each others life. I filled like I could move away from the situation. Well, at least a little bit. I had to. I had my own problems.

During my years in Walla Walla, I felt like I was a victim of hate crimes on so many different levels. Verbal and physical abuse by people I did and didn't know all based on something they either assumed, thought they knew or wanted to judge about my sexuality.

For the most part, I tried to be as strong as possible but one night I had pushed my sexuality too far into too many faces. I was living about two miles from school and would bike back and forth several times a day. It was my senior year I was living alone but in the same building as Terra and David. I had been working late in the art studio. It was about eleven and decided to bike home.

About a mile into it I felt like I was being stalked from afar. I was being watched. There was a wide, low riding, red Plymouth following me with six men inside. I could tell immediately they didn't go to the college just from the car, the way they talked, and what they wore. They all wore the tattoo of one of the meth gangs on the east side. I tried to bike faster and started heading up on the grass, but the driver got so close that he knocked against my back wheel with his right headlight. My bike tipped over. They started throwing beer cans at me and then got out of the car. I left it there and started running, but it was too late. I had no chance. They all started kicking me in the ribs and slapping me in the face. They were all yelling out "bull dyke", "bull dagger", "muff muncher" or even "taco bumper". There were worse comments but you're getting the idea. The leader of the crew yelled out to get the hammer. I was screaming as loud as I could. But no one was going to take a chance and help me. I saw several curtains get closed.

Cheap alcohol was wafting from their clothes. Two of them held my left hand down to the ground as the driver beat it with a hammer until my entire wrist was shattered. I couldn't fight them anymore. I had been kicked so many times that I was coughing up blood. I finally either scared them or bored them. I lay their screaming for help but no one was willing. They didn't even have to approach me. A quick call to 911 would have been sufficient enough.

I remember looking across the street and there were the steps to a local church. Weren't we all supposed to be children of God? If he actually did exist would he have let this happen? Wasn't God was supposed to be watching over me?

I couldn't help it. All I could think was that he must be a gang banging meth head himself and was riding a good high that night. Or rather, he clearly does not exist. Prayer surely wasn't going to help me. The only thing I could think to do was to try to bike back home, tell Terra and David, and call the police. The police arrived thirty minutes later to say there was nothing they could do. They refused to take my statement, which made me think that they were probably part of the same gang themselves. When I arrived at the hospital I was told that in the state of Washington if you are a victim of a hate crime your medical care is free. They gave me an arm cast and bound my ribs. The doctor told me that this was my fault because I was different and that I should give "normal" things more of a try. He wouldn't even make eye contact with me and put on gloves to shake my hand.

Once I realized my connection with art, I took every class possible. I had gone into college with such a plan as to what I would major in and accomplish, but it was time for a change. I had a new found ambition. For my entire senior year, I did my art thesis on hate crimes against lesbians, gays, bisexuals, and transgendered individuals. In my art, I depicted the trauma, viciousness, and horror of anti-gay violence through my own eyes and experiences. The main issue I addressed was documenting victimization, the social consequences of bigotry and bashing, violence against lesbians, and the emotional consequences of anti-gay violence.

There have always been artists who were lesbians and lesbians who were artists, but the category "lesbian artist" scarcely existed before 1970. What is a lesbian artist? The natural response is someone who makes lesbian art. But there is no agreement about what constitutes lesbian art, though generally it is thought to reflect the lesbian identity and to contribute to the development of that identity. At that point in time, upon looking in the mirror I was confronted by a condition to which I was bound. Without the desire to modify my current condition I was forced to face my face. I felt I must find a way to set down a record of it, to process it through the creation of art. My goal was to avoid what many artists have done, masterfully creating masks of themselves, but rather provided a self-unveiling for the viewer.

Every year Whitman gives out the David Nord Award, which is given to one student a year who focuses on homosexual issues through their thesis. I wrote my proposal and won the award. They gave me three thousand dollars to use towards making my project everything I dreamed it to be. At the end of the year, I had to give a speech about what I had been doing that year but it wasn't hard. We had to do this every week in art class anyway. I was certainly honored to receive the award. That year my art was then given third place for most innovative project in the Northwest. . I also had my thesis published in CALYX, a journal of art and literature by women. I exhibited at various wineries, many small Washington galleries, and even at the University of Washington and Oregon. My best and most frequent buyer was actually the manager of the bookshop at the college. Every month he would buy something new from me. I think

Keiko convinced him they would be worth something someday.

My psychology thesis is simpler to explain. I was studying the cause and impact of having a fragmented self, not being whole. This is not to be confused with having Dissociative Identity Disorder or Multiple Personality disorder, as most people know it. This disorder is extremely rare, where fragmenting and compartmentalizing is something most people do to cope at some point in their lives. Whether you become fragmented through trauma or a disorder or just genetics it splits your personality making it hard to become fulfilled. To become a whole person again seems impossible. But many people subconsciously, fragment their personalities without even knowing they are doing it almost as a way to protect themselves.

The Washington State Penitentiary was less then a mile from campus, which provided me with a whole education in itself. One of the psychology courses we had to take was basically an internship working with the psychiatry department of the prison. This prison handled all of the executions for the state. I worked in the High Crime Facility, which only handles those facing life sentences without a chance of parole or death row. I would sit in on weekly appointments between those on death row and their psychiatrist.

But this was not for therapy, it was for research.

The doctor would often start each appointment trying to tap into any feelings of depression, guilt, or shame. The inmate was asked to explain in detail about particulars of their crime, but this was always a failure. To truly think about what they did and the feelings they had seemed impossible for the inmates. Often questions would result in evil or maniacal laughter. Just like in comic books when the super-villains utter such laughs. It would mean that they would have to be honest with themselves, not just about their actions, but who they really are. This resulted in the fragmentation of self.

The other way each of them handled this situation was to begin to brag about what they had done. Often in an attempt to make their case seem more extravagant then the next guys inhumane crimes. For example, more victims, increased brutality, and eluding the police in some kind of clever cat and mouse game gave each of them perceived increased status within the prison walls. After all, they were specialists at making viciousness into art. It was obvious that using such hyperboles made them feel better about themselves. This created an entirely new identity where their criminal act was now seen as something to be desired. They had nothing left to lose and so they felt they should and could say anything, do anything, without any repercussions. After all they had been in locked seclusion for years. How much worse could it get for them? They needed a way to feel strong. It is dangerous. Power is so intoxicating. Deceit was the main goal.

It appeared on the outside that I was actually doing well. But my academic successes were just the outside shell. The story told without the guts.

~ Eleven ~

The summer before my senior year of college I decided to go live with Eva outside Los Angeles. I had a prestigious advertising and graphic design internship in Pasadena, companionship, and a place to live. It seemed like a great choice for the summer before my senior year of college. A few days after arriving, I remember sitting on the toilet and thinking this is a moment when everything is perfect. Had this ever happened before? I pushed my toes into the pink coral rug holding on to time. But that was just what it was – a moment.

Two weeks into what seemed like it would be the best summer of my life, I woke up with intense pain in my stomach. I quickly told my girlfriend that I needed to see a doctor. Since I didn't live in the area, I didn't have a physician that I saw regularly or ever. After a trip to a strip mall doctor cost me seventy-five dollars cash for his opinion that I needed to see someone else, I went to the nearest emergency room, Chino Medical Center, where it was determined that I needed an immediate appendectomy. I called my mother to let her know. Mostly I called because I was under her insurance but more to let her know it wasn't anything serious and that I didn't want her to come out. My girlfriend and my mother had never gotten along and I knew that they would not be able to work together and to set aside their differences while I was in surgery.

I knew that for a while I would not be able to help the situation to the best of my ability. So before my surgery, I sat down with two nurses and the head of security to do the necessary paperwork which stated that if my mother was to come in the building or if she calls that she is not to be given any information about my health status or to be let in my room. I made it clear that security was to remove her from the hospital. Even though I may have looked young, I was an adult. They were going to protect me while I was down for the count. I needed to be sure of it.

Unfortunately, my appendix wasn't the problem. Two incisions and nine staples later my perfect appendix lay in medical waste thanks to a nervous interns quick interpretation and his antique approach to slicing me open. Instead of the modern laparoscopy technique this idiot left me with three scars. One that goes across half my stomach and is about a foot long. Just what a young women wants. And at the time I wasn't overweight either. There was no reason for this to happen. I woke up in more intense pain then before. Several fools scrambled around scratching their head and twirling their hair trying to appear interested. They pushed at my freshly cut belly without washing their hands. My screams just made them more frantic. Not knowing anything, they determined an ultrasound would figure it out. It revealed that I had four orange sized cysts all over my ovaries. One had just exploded while they were poking around. Before the anesthesia had worn off I was being rolled into my second surgery.

But when I woke up my mother was lying in a cot next to my hospital bed. If had been able to move, I could have rolled right on top of her she was so close. She had also told them that I was lying about a rare, life threatening blood pressure condition that I had and told them to take me off the medicine that I had been receiving. Within fifteen minutes of waking up, all the anxiety combined with being without my medication cause me to have a heart attack at age twenty. The fact that she caused this to happen to me just because she wanted to have control was so cruel and twisted. She was so manipulative even the hospital wouldn't listen to my instructions that I left before my surgery. I told my mother that I never wanted to see or talk to her again and I had security escort her out of the building. I immediately revoked my financial power of attorney. That was the last time I spoke to her.

Eva was so pissed that I had supposedly endangered her life by allowing my mother to be there that she wouldn't even come to pick me up. I still was unable to care for myself and I had no place to go. So without me even asking Eva's mother flew out to California to pick me up from the hospital and brought me to Eva's empty apartment. Eva had flown all the way back to Maine to avoid me. But her mother watched over me for two weeks until I was able to move back to Walla Walla on my own.

The day I moved in Eva called to say that she was dumping

me because I didn't protect her from my mother when I was having surgery. You would think that in a time when I had two surgeries and an unnecessary heart attack she could have actually stuck up for me for once. But no, she was done with me. It wasn't exactly a surprise since we hardly we talking at this point, but it still sank me to another low.

I needed to make this work. Since I was no longer speaking to any family except for my grandfather, who I did not want to take advantage of, I got three jobs right away. I found a small studio apartment about two miles away from school. I had no money after paying the security deposit on my apartment. I knew my grandfather would help if I asked, but I desperately wanted to show him that I could be independent. I would starve to death before I would ever take one cent from my mother.

How was I going to make enough money to support myself and still graduate on time? My friends suggested I drop one of my degrees, but I wasn't about to give up on my education. I got three jobs as soon as I could. I was already the Manager of the Digital Media Lab at the College. Then the School and Event Advertising Department hired me on to design and photograph for their college catalogues they constantly put out, and to do a media package for all paid guests of the college. The least glamorous of the three was working in the payroll office early in the morning before classes started. This all made it so I could pay the rent, bills, and food. I often would eat at the college when I would be low on money because they had to feed me. I carefully counted each penny. I never had anything extra but it didn't matter. What else did I really need?

I bought all my groceries at this discount Mexican grocer. The only catch was you had to speak Spanish. The stock was always changing so you might not be able to find your item the next week. Everything in the store was dented or spelt wrong on the box. I didn't care how the packaging looked as long as it wasn't expired and tasted good. The bread was usually a day old but it was still moderately fresh. I was able buy food for the week for about thirty dollars.

I felt myself turning inward more and more. The louder the voices got the less I liked being around other people. More and more I wanted to be by myself so I could carry out the compulsions of my illness without being judged. I didn't want to realize yet how much I needed help.

This was the first time I had never had a roommate. The first year I was living with Andi, the ignorant bitch, and then the next was a positive experience with my good friend Kate. The third year Terra and I rented this huge apartment near the school. It had two bedrooms, high ceilings and hardwood floors. It was only three hundred and fifty dollars a month including utilities. Someone was there to keep me clean, organized, and in line.

My final year, Terra lived in a separate apartment in the same building, but even though she was so close it didn't prevent my advancing destruction. I noticed that very rapidly I was unable to care for myself. I couldn't keep organized. The only thing it seemed I could do was to obsess over the mailman's coming and goings. I would neglect my appearance because I the thought of it was too overwhelming. My apartment was a disaster area. I was barely eating and all I did was paint in my room. I was so lonely and scared of others at the same time. I didn't know how to make this all work. I had no coping skills for my growing symptoms. Occasionally, I would visit Terra and David who lived in the basement apartment or see other friends at their place but no one ever came to visit me. I didn't really want them there anyway. I was off in my own world. I had an increasing amount of people to watch out my window.

I had a cat I called Pie. He chewed every cord in my house so I ended up having hardly any power. My radio and TV didn't work. But

I cared for Pie. I rescued him from the street. He was so malnourished. I couldn't help but take him home. I made sure he was never hungry and had his shots. I took better care of him than myself. I spend most days watching cars, people, and patterns. I was starting to lose time. I felt like I was being sucked into a black hole.

Luckily, free health care was included with tuition. Baskets of condoms and antibiotics were in constant demand. The only ones who knew this included your mental health were struggling like me. I had already been experiencing audio and visual hallucinations for more than four years, but now they were taking over my life. My once perfect grades took a dive. I was separating myself from my own reality. I desperately needed more than the support of my friends. I needed professional help and medication. The appointments took place in a separate location than the health center in the basement of the administration building. I was completely unaware that it had become so obvious to those around me until my concerned advisor walked me down the stairs to my first appointment.

Since the campus included many eye-catching ponds and streams the ducks had found paradise. They stayed there and multiplied until there were so many that the majority were put into a truck once a year and driven to some other location to avoid over crowding. They are cute until they bite the backs of your ankles while you walk and steal your lunch. I am a big animal lover. They were bullies.

The short stairwell was on the side of the building. It was what everyone called, "Duck Rape Alley" during springs mating season. The males would push the females down the cement steps, hop on their back and bite their neck until she screamed. Then he would leave her used up at the bottom while he left with his chest puffed out.

I felt like I had two choices to either wander my way through duck rape alley or get admitted to St. Mary's Hospital right down the street.

So I climbed down the stairs to the small office filled with staff I had never seen all in sweater vests. I would try to sneak down the steps and push my way in through the heavy metal door before I thought anyone could see. Some how living under the delusion that an appointment with a therapist would be more embarrassing then talking to myself or screaming at no one. Almost immediately I was given a diagnosis and put on drugs.

My first psychotherapist, Dr. Amiri, was a late thirty

something single ex heroin user turned healer. He always wore his sunglasses always on top of his curly, greasy hair. He would tell me stories about searching the streets and looking for his next fix. He used to say he did it for the same reasons I cut up my arms. We both wanted to mask emotional pain. It was somewhat of an okay analogy, but in reality he probably used his shooting up to relate to all of his patients. The thing was that none of his patients were drug addicts and he wasn't an interventionist, so it seemed to me that he needed another technique. Whenever he would talk about getting high he would tap the lower part off his arm with two straightened stuck together fingers. The more he did it the more ridiculous it seemed. I wasn't able to connect with him in any way.

He talked so quickly and constantly I hardly had to say a thing. I guess it was a good thing considering I am so quiet. Most of the time I would just see if he was trying to read my mind. But then I would just block him out. I had too much else going on with myself before I could begin to sympathize with his fifteen-year addiction.

At first, he thought maybe it was Post Traumatic Stress Disorder from some disturbing episode earlier in life. The go to diagnosis for people who have odd behaviors because everyone has had trauma on some level in their life. PTSD has become a catch phrase that so many people throw out there without really knowing what it means.

I really I didn't care what my label was. I just wanted help. But I was sure of one thing hallucinations and delusions are not part of your garden variety of PTSD. I may have been the patient, but I knew I was psychotic. I was losing whole parts of my day. The disorder was causing people to think I was lying because I had a different memory than they did. Or I had a delusion that I would tell my friends and then would laugh at me and ask why would I make up such stupid stories. Or they would believe me and then later accuse me of lying. Honestly, it pissed me off because I felt like no one believed my reality or me. I felt like I was losing myself. Where was I going? I mean if I say it happened then it did. I wasn't lying. I fully believed what I was experiencing and telling everyone. Only now can I do some differentiating thanks to my psychiatrists and those I trust, including my Chihuahua Liam. People will say to me, just think it through. Rationally, does this really make sense? Use your mind. But that is just the problem. I can't use my mind to fix the problem when my mind is the problem. It is broken.

Twisted shivered secrets watched by the frozen dragon. Unfold dragon. Chill wind only wastes fate. Feel bathed magic yawn.

Azure joy answers. Prisoner devours yesterday's poison. Morning throbs with naked velvet. Melt rhythm and surround your porcelain lie. Perhaps your secret self is home. Speak steal smoke and surround time, linger so when the window opens you are not left naked.

Which thoughts should come out and when? Will any of this make sense?

Since he was just a therapist, he was determined I needed to see the one psychiatrists they had for those who needed prescription medication. The psychiatrist was of those women that had just turned fifty and had a metal rod implanted directly up her ass. She didn't feel they were paying her enough to care. There was no understanding, no listening, and she surely didn't make an effort to know you or your name. All you were to her was a manila folder. She would read back to you what your psychologist thought. At first, I figured this was for my benefit because it appeared therapeutic but in reality she read it out loud at that moment because she hadn't bothered to read it before the appointment. And then she would always say, "So you are feeling better, right? Right???" If you said, "Actually no, I am not feeling better." She would flatly laugh lightly without emotion and continue on no matter what you said or she had just read about your current behaviors. Then she would write out some prescription without much explanation to why you were taking it or what it would do. She was so cold hearted you could feel the boundary that was around her to keep you at a certain distance.

"Have you ever taken these before?" I remember quickly shaking my head, suddenly being more embarrassed because of the hushed voice of the pharmacist then the medication itself. He looked around as if filling this prescription would make others think he needed them. "It can be dangerous. Make sure to read the information before you take any." I looked like a deer stuck in the headlights. I was going through the motions to receive help but I didn't know yet if I really wanted it. Would I even take these pills? What were they trying to do to me?

I already felt mortified. How would I tell my friends or would I? Somehow telling people I have schizoaffective disorder became more difficult than coming out of the closet. Which isn't an easy thing to say, but at that moment it felt true. I tried to tell Eva what the doctors were saying, but she would always say that she didn't want to talk about that. That I was too smart to be crazy, she didn't believe it, and that it was just something I was making up. I tried to explain to her that I had a disease that could be treated but not cured. And that if I had cancer she wouldn't accuse me of lying or say I should be able to take care of this on my own. She never wanted to hear any of it.

I was craving human affection. No, not sex, I just wanted a hug. Something. Even a tap on the shoulder. It is amazing how weird it feels when it has been too long. Shame had completely invaded my heart, mind, and soul. All she wanted to know was that I was getting help, but not what for. I wanted to tell her so she would have some answers. I was also trying to have some support. Mental illness is so lonely. I thought maybe she could read a book about what was going on with me. But that never happened. If it had I don't think our relationship would have fell apart like it did.

After trying to live on my own for about half a year, I began to notice that things were starting to go downhill quickly. I never felt like I could vacuum, or do the dishes, or even bother to pick up my clothes on the floor. It is hard to explain and most would say I was lazy but that's not it. I just literally felt like I couldn't do it. Like I didn't know how anymore. I was just struggling with the small tasks that are involved in taking care of oneself. I didn't get help because I wanted to. It seemed like I needed to. I didn't want to do most. I felt frozen. At the same time, I was holding down three jobs, paying all my own bills, and receiving two complete Bachelor degrees in just four years. So maybe I just can't think about anything like cleaning when I have all that going on, right? Why didn't anyone think about that? But looking back, this train of thought was just there to not make me feel like a total degenerate. It wasn't the answer.

I looked up hallucinations on the Internet. I was hoping to find some answers, a way to connect, and not to feel so alone. What I found were a bunch of people joking and glamorizing about hallucinations. As if it was like tripping on mushrooms. Comments mostly consisted of "how cool it was" or "I can't wait for it to happen again" or "schizophrenics are so lucky". I threw the laptop across the room. It all pissed me off. People like this are exactly why the mental health community has so little support and empathy.

I sat at my kitchen table staring at the orange bottle. I had read the print out given to me by the pharmacist six times. Side effects may include stiff (rigid) muscles, high fever, sweating, confusion, fast or uneven heartbeats, tremors; feeling like you might pass out; jerky muscle movements you cannot control that may be permanent, trouble swallowing, problems with speech; tremors, or restless muscle movements in your eyes, tongue, jaw, neck, arms, or legs; along with many other "less serious" side effects. A panic attack ensued. But it wasn't the exaggerated "When I saw the electricity bill I just had a panic attack!" Or, "I had a panic attack when I woke up and saw I was two hours late for work." Few people know how a panic attack actually feels unless you've actually had one.

The palpitations began as if a June bug had crawled into my mouth running its legs over my taste buds. You can feel it, building like an unstoppable snowball in the pit of your stomach. At first I just hope it's a dodgy stomach or indigestion, but my negative brain latches on to it, making me think, and procrastinate on the slight unrest in my stomach. I start thinking about the feeling in my stomach uncontrollably, nothing can stop me prodding and poking it with my mind, swirling it ever faster.

I cannot concentrate on anything else that I'm doing. I just sit and wallow in the feeling and how I know it will escalate into panic. I don't know why I am so certain that the panic will ensue. I suppose it's because it has always happened in the past. Past behavior is the best predictor of future behavior. I can no longer regulate my breathing. The air in the room has all been sucked out. The only way I've found to stop it happening is to not let it get to that stage of no return, but without help this seems impossible. The next step is my heart starting to beat harder and faster, adrenaline levels rise, bugs crawl up inside my body and my brain starts to fire out negative thoughts like a machine gun. I wouldn't call them hallucinations, but they are very strong visions (almost out of body) where I see myself being out of control with panic, crying, falling to the floor, upsetting and confusing everyone around me. I believe these visions are the future and that this will definitely happen and nothing I can do will stop it. A sweat starts to happen all over the body. It feels like your skin has another hot skin on the outside. It moves over your body and never releases. Just round and round until you feel microwaved.

The negative thoughts keep coming like waves on rocks. I start projecting my feelings into the future. I start a fight with feelings of never being able to go outside, being fired, not being able to afford the rent, being a terrible friend by not being able to keep sane when everyone is there to help, being ridiculed by friends and being taken away for being utterly useless. The visions are so real that at the time I have no doubt that all these worst case scenarios most certainly will come true. Every single one will happen.

At this point I cannot just sit still, I start pacing or moving around irrationally. Taking two steps towards something then recoiling as I start having negative thoughts about those actions. For instance thinking about going outside will help, but that means going to the door. I could head for the door, but what if people are in the garden, I don't want them to see me, but I can't stay here it's making me feel ill, but outside might make me feel worse. I am trapped constantly in a world of darkness. Where the hell is that? It's counter argument after counter argument. They are all utterly ridiculous and futile but very real when I am panicking. I cannot make up my mind as there are at least two minds trying to kick each other in. I feel completely trapped by my brain. My vision is blurred and chaotic.

The next step is the worst. The arguments in my head get so rapid and so disturbing that my brain shuts down my body. I can no longer cope with the thoughts and feelings in my head and body. I fall to the floor, fully conscious but unable to stop what is happening. The sweat has completely covered my body and my heart feels like it's going to explode. I can see but the world is not like it should be. Like everything I see has peeled itself away from reality and now exists in a sort of fantasy world. I cannot move or speak for fear of the fear. The only thing to do is to wait for enough adrenaline to be created so that I can get up and run to safety.

At the very worst points of these panic attacks, I want the ground to open up and swallow me. It's odd; I don't think about killing myself, I don't want to give that impression. I just wish that I never existed in the first place so that my sorry state isn't a burden on myself or anyone else anymore. I feel so beaten up I am unable to perform basic tasks causing me to feel like a failure of a human being. Simply, I am a waste of a life.

I think that restricting myself to routines that were successful makes me think that the panic attack won't happen if I just stick to the routine. If I eat the same cereal, if I go the same way to work, with the same people, do the same amount of work, in the same way, in the same place, go home the same way, and do the same things when I get back that I will be safe. Then as it worked yesterday, it should work today without stressing me out. But it is not that easy.

Zyprexa was the first drug trial. They started me on a low dose of 5mg at first and then moved me up to 20mg. I remember when the pharmacist handed me my first prescription he warned me of all the horrible side effects and recommended that I have someone sleep at my apartment the first night just in case. Just in case what? Yea, that's what I wanted to know but he wouldn't go into details. I felt like I had no choice. So I took my first antipsychotic with Terra sleeping over for the night just in case. It put me to sleep quickly which was the only good part about it.

The next morning when I finally woke It made me feel physically paralyzed, but mentally I was screaming inside. My speech had become slow and stammering. It was hard to move or talk. My brain felt completely rewired. Numbed in a bad way. I was flooded some of the most bizarre side effects. I felt like I was even more separated from reality. I put my hand up to my face and it felt like I was touching someone else. It was like I was watching everything around me happen in slow motion to those around me and no one could see me. I was just an observer. I was moving through glue. I was so tired. My body was restless, crawling with ants. But I couldn't move as much as I felt like I needed to because I felt like I was partially paralyzed.

Weeks later Terra felt like I was gone and someone else had taken over my body. It felt like my voice had been taken away. My friends all asked the same question; where did I go? So this was my choice? I was losing myself either way to the medication or the illness. I struggle with this decision today. Was this Invasion of The Body Snatchers? Eventually most of the nasty feelings dissipate but I don't believe for a second that anyone likes taking antipsychotics. Truth is that I still have hallucinations. Every day.

What part of our life is under our control? What if we choose to live a life that is only of our own making? Would this save us from despair? Living in your own delusion would be the triumph of irrationality.

Is either a way that someone should be forced to live? I stay at home watching that man still walk up and down my street. How did he get here? Want does he want? Everyday thirty-two minutes I see him. I resort to flicking the light switch on and off seven times. Now he knows someone is home. Please stay away. At least he doesn't have a key. I have been sprayed in a hard resin shell. I have been covered by colors, numbers, and static. I am frozen in my own time.

Maybe I have been poisoned without knowing it. These headaches and the voices progress further and further. Maybe there was a curing drink or a needle that is the deliverer of the end. I can't just have a normal day anymore. My brain is under attack. Who and what can stop these headaches? Or who can stop it all? The man was at the restaurant this afternoon.

My workload had become too much for me to handle. My head was all jumped up with the voices of Larry and Maggie fighting with my antipsychotics and what was left of me. I'm not sure I can leave the house today. I'm petrified that the man will be there and then what do I do. Invite him in the house? No. I guess I won't have to because he will probably come in on his own. I'm so scared. I'm getting worse. I can barely breathe. Young worry streams down the window while ferocious fire haunts perpetual memory. Don't waste time chasing eternal concrete

My bed is the only place that I feel safe. He followed me in a blue car all the way home. The motor kept sputtering. I heard him say his name is Larry to someone the other day. But why are you following me Larry? Who do you work for? I am too scared to ask him. I don't want any more people coming to get me. I just need advice because Larry is telling me if I cut he will escape my body and not bother me anymore.

All the while, I was still finishing my degrees. I graduated with a bachelors degree in studio art and psychology with a minor in gay and lesbian studies in four years. I appeared successful.

Two days before my college graduation I went to let Pie, my cat, back inside, and my mother was sitting right there on the floor in front of my door. She wasn't invited, I hadn't talked to her in almost a year, and she didn't even knock. It scared me shitless. I slammed the door shut and locked it immediately. What was she doing here? What the hell did she want from me? I wasn't going to let myself be part of her game anymore. With the door shut, I told her if she didn't leave in five minutes that I would call the police. I had a already gotten restraining order against her when I stopped talking to her at the hospital. She begged and pleaded for me to let her in. I called the cops and she was escorted out of the building. After a while, when I opened my door, I saw a pile of stuff on the floor. A bank book that she had taken all the money out off but three dollars and twelve cents, Along with a few bonds that my grandmother had left me years before. What was this supposed to be? A bribe?

Afterwards I immediately called Eva. Despite our broken up status we talked pretty much every night for a couple hours. I told her what had happened. We were supposed to still be friends after all. BIG mistake. She became more paranoid than I was and she lived over one thousand miles away. At one point during the conversation I said her name. Something like, "Eva it's over, it's going to be okay." And she flipped. She said what if my mother was standing outside my door again and heard me saying her name. She didn't want to talk to me just in case my mother heard me say her name through the wall. She thought that somehow that would cause my mother to go after her. So irrational. She said I was endangering her life by simply saying her name when no one was there. At the time I fell for it. I did.

I somehow tried to understand where she was coming from. But now, I know how incredibly absurd all of this was.

Due to the entire situation and not knowing if my mother was still in town, which I figured she was I cried. I cried until my whole body was shaking. I cried for the two days while I was attempting to move out to fly back to Maine until my graduation My eyelids were so puffy I could barely open my eyes. I wept until no more tears could come out. In the process of moving out, I was getting rid of anything I couldn't fit into two suitcases, except for some of my artwork, which I did ship. I saw no point in saving junk to only end up carrying it around the country. I gave all my furniture to a thrift shop in town. They moved it our for free as long as I didn't want anything for it. I had decided to fly to my Grandpa's house. I had no other choice really. Plus, I need desperately to be around someone who truly loved me. So while I spent all those days crying and crying I was also sleeping on the floor with a sweatshirt for a pillow.

My graduation had turned into rock bottom. When it came time to put my graduation outfit on it should have been one of the proudest moments of my life but my eyes ached, everyone looked at me funny, and I was constantly worried my mother was there hiding somewhere in the audience.

I graduated summa cum laude with seven other students. The best part was that when I walked up to get my diploma as I shook the president's hand he told me he wanted to buy my entire thesis and have it as a permanent collection in the library. I felt so honored that he had even paid attention to what I was doing and even more so that he believed in what I was trying to accomplish. For a moment I stepped out of my head. I was so proud that I barely cared about the diploma in my hands.

I flew back to Maine. The plane spreads its wings; a mosaic of symbolic dreams and the moon's happiness ironically fulfilled men of evil desire. Once walked so high, now walk so low. Twenty-nine sparrows come to take my soul; twenty-nine sparrows come to take my soul. Those evil brilliant monkeys on the prowl and whisper in the woods so that I can hear them growl. Seek refinement, Seek refinement. Gonna drop off these shores. Don't want it no more. Down on the fence post and up the walk. Monkeys and birds all plan to stalk. Chains on my ankles, a stylish clink all I induce is an invisible shrink. Can't block it no more. I see no winner. Tolerance is bothersome, who is the sinner. Throw skulls down the tunnel with no control. Take a fire walk with me. The voices are telepathic animals. Tweet tweet isn't life sweet?

Intertwining, ever lining, rearranging and defining upside in and outside down Mozart's requiem, no sound. But louder as it changes pace in place of the space it fills the vase. And flowers blooming over flow, but your minds so big that it implodes. Tiny specs float into air. A grid a myriad through her hair and juxtaposed to fit the mold your brain slides back to crease and fold. I must stitch it up, but not too tight after all it is our right and we must add some glitter add some glue. Some pills will make you good as new but sometimes they scrutinize through lying eyes that fill the room, which you despise. Sedated in the padded cell you go to scream but no one can hear me. I am all alone. Obtrusive thoughts skewed by projection. Astral in all it's affection and lucid dreams to keep the time but isn't it all in my mind?

~ Twelve ~

That summer, immediately after arriving at my grandfathers house, he showed me a clipping from the newspaper. The house I grew up in, which was technically half mine, had been sold by my mother showing an out of date copy of the power of attorney and committing fraud by forging my name on the real estate documents. My mother sold the house I grew up in which was half mine by using my any manipulative way she knew how without my knowledge or agreement. Following this there were many financial indiscretions that came into light, which included taking my checking account to pay for her fiancés couples counseling with his soon to be ex-wife two months after my father died, and renting and living in our other property without my consent. This all led to an eight-year probate court lawsuit against my mother to receive the money that I should have gotten from my fathers estate because she went against her fiduciary duty as my financial power of attorney.

When my grandfather showed me a picture of my sold house in the local paper he was so pissed. At the time, I think he was more upset than I was about what happened but I had been trying to turn off my emotions for some time. After I completely digested what was happening, I was fully on board. I wasn't focused on revenge or making her life a living hell. It was then I realized I wasn't after revenge at all. I just wanted to get back what was legally mine and to have a home of my own at the end of all this. I wanted to do something about it, but I didn't have any money for a lawyer. I felt like there was nothing I could do. But without me even asking, my grandfather told me to call his lawyer. She gave me a recommendation of one of the best probate lawyers in the county.

Unfortunately, I picked her second choice at first because I was trying to save my grandfather some money.

Soon after arriving back home, I moved in to Eva's house with her parents. I wanted to move on and be happy like we used to now that we were finally living in the same place again. But you can never have the past back. Unfortunately, it became more and more rocky. Her OCD (Obsessive Compulsive Disorder) was progressing rapidly and there was nothing I could do that she didn't believe would hurt her. She tried meds and therapy but it was impossible to stop this in time before it all crashed. I think part of her liked how her disorder caused people to quickly back down, be a little scared, and let her get whatever she wanted. She felt like she was in control.

For example, if I dropped something, even a pencil, and then picked it up and set it back on the table I would have brought the germs from the floor onto my hands and onto the table where she might eat. But it got worse. Soon she considered me so contaminated I couldn't even touch her, kiss her, not anything. There was no trust.

Technically we were separated. Just friends. Like that always works. And that was what I wanted. But she was always pushing the boundaries, which for the most part was hard to resist. All the lines were blurred.

Her parents had always loved me and appreciated me from the start. Her mother is an amazing opera singer. She would always sing while cooking dinner and we would go to watch her perform here and there. She was a very strong woman and I looked up to her. Her father was the business owner of his own accounting firm. In the beginning, they were always on a tight budget, but things quickly changed. They made me feel like I actually had a family again. The first winter there they gave me my own embroidered stocking with my name on it to hang with every one else's above the fireplace. I couldn't help but cry. I was so happy. Her father and mother never cared that I was a girl dating her girl. Somehow I think they were happy they knew there daughter was safe and that I wouldn't take advantage.

They were well off and have this beautiful renovated farmhouse with plenty of land. Once her father's mother passed away he received millions of dollars in inheritance. And Eva and her brother both more than most people make their entire lives. Things changed rapidly. Paying over one hundred dollars each for dinner was the norm.

They had a sleek sailboat. Over the years they moved up and up in class until they had a magnificent forty-eight foot boat. Every summer since Eva and I were ten years old, before we were dating, we would coast down east or from Portland down to Newport, Rhode Island. We would stop and take our time. They taught me how to steer, read the maps, talk on the radio, pull in the sails, check the depth, and dock the boat. I loved the experience. Over the years, we had stayed at every harbor available in New England.

When I was at their house they allowed me to treat it like mine as long as I kept it clean; in the same shape that it was left in. At the time, I had gotten back on my medicine so I was particularly good at this. I did not want to upset them. They had done do much for me. I hoped someday I could help out someone like they helped me. Sometimes, when Eva and I were having a difficult time I would go downstairs to talk to her mother. I would just leave her alone for at least an hour and just see then what she could do on her own. I didn't know who else to go to. No matter how overwhelmed I was she always understood and made me feel better. Without going against her daughter, she made me feel understood. She told me I didn't deserve to be treated like I was and if I decided to leave she would always be there for me in my life. I couldn't have had better in-laws. She knew her daughter better than I did so she completely got where I was coming from.

Eva had to have serious foot surgery because she had flat feet all her life, which was increasingly very painful. Plus, her weight was getting higher and putting more pressure on her ankles. They basically had to break and replace the position of almost every bone on her foot. The podiatrist said it could only be done one foot at a time and it will take almost a year to recover for each foot. At the same time she found out she had borderline type II diabetes. I decided I would help her through the whole process. Dressing, showering, and toileting. You name it.

We stayed in separate rooms side by side so we could have our own space so I gave her a bell. Whatever the hour was she would ring that damn thing. At first, I figured it would just be used to wake me if she had to go to the bathroom in the night, but eventually it was "I'm hungry" at three am or "I don't like these socks can you get me new ones" which was often in the middle of the night. Her parents stayed in a separate part of the house safe away from the ringing madness. I know they couldn't have dealt with what I was going through. Looking back she wasn't necessarily even appreciating how much I was constantly doing. She was using me.

One day we drove home and before we got out of the car she noticed her dad dragging a shovel behind him along the driveway.

She said that the entire driveway was cross contaminated with germs and that she wouldn't get out until the whole driveway, which wasn't small, was cleaned with bleach. I kept saying to her parents to, please, not clean the driveway. I wanted to make her get out of the car, and finally, face all the fear she had inside.

Obsessive-compulsive disorder is an anxiety disorder characterized by uncontrollable, unwanted thoughts and repetitive, ritualized behaviors you feel compelled to perform. If you have OCD, you probably recognize that your obsessive thoughts and compulsive behaviors are irrational – but even so, you feel unable to resist them and break free. Like a needle getting stuck on an old record, OCD causes the brain to get stuck on a particular thought or urge. For example, you may check the stove twenty times to make sure it's really turned off, wash your hands until they're scrubbed raw, or drive around for hours to make sure that the bump you heard while driving wasn't a person you ran over.

They were not helping her. But they did it anyway. Six gallons of bleach later and she got out of the car.

There were special ways I had to use the bathroom. After I finished, I couldn't touch or pull up my pants. I had to waddle to the sink, wash my hands in the proper way, and then pull up my pants because if I had touched them before I washed them they would be contaminated from wiping myself. So if I would touch the waist of my pants later in the day, all she could think was "you pulled up your pants before you washed your hands, didn't you?" She would listen at the bathroom door to make sure I was doing everything correctly in the proper way. It's crazy thinking back on it. It felt like I had OCD because just like her I was living with it. I had to follow in line with her behaviors so she would feel better. But I wasn't really helping her either.

Once I was sick in the hospital and she came to visit. Some hippy doctor told her she might have some problem from being in a public place with certain bacteria which most people have without even knowing, but it goes away quickly without treatment. Of course, she figured I must have caused it because I was in the hospital and she never should have gone. That it was my fault. I tried my best but it felt so overwhelming. I had to put my legs through my underwear without my feet touching anywhere on the fabric because then I was dirty. I became so polluted to her that she wouldn't ever touch me even after a shower. Everyone became the enemy and it now included me.

Sometimes, things would get very tough.

At that time, everything was about her and because of her OCD she became very manipulative to get what she compulsively needed. She used it as an excuse for this behavior or action. I never heard a single "I'm sorry". There was never any compromise. It never occurred to her that the relationship should be two sided. They tell you to separate the behavior from the person, but that is easier than it sounds. It all felt like it didn't matter how hard I tried. I had to give up who I was and become the behavior as well if I wanted to stay in her life. It was getting progressively worse. I always think that if I had known more about the disorder and cognitive behavioral therapy at the time that maybe, just maybe, I could have helped her a little bit. But I was too close to her. She needed someone that she didn't know to give her a symbolic slap on the face and tell her to get on with her life.

I also started us both on the South Beach Diet and cooked every meal from scratch. I was so busy. Plus, her doctor had told her she was slightly allergic to seven different foods so I had to read every single label very carefully. They were yeast, chicken, carrots, nuts, aluminum, mushrooms, and corn. If I messed up just once, she kicked me out. I would leave until she realized she needed me again. I was completely whipped and I let it happen. She only would bring me back because she needed my help. Caring for her, someone to put up with her OCD, shopping, cooking, and pushing her wheelchair when she wanted to go on walks together. Because of all the exercise and change in eating, I quickly lost over seventy pounds in just three months.

Once I started seeing her able to walk and do things on her own I realized she didn't need me anymore. I desperately needed to not need her. She would sneak into the kitchen to get a midnight snack when she thought I wasn't paying attention. And then an hour later she would be ringing her bell repeatedly because she wanted a drink. I wasn't going to be made a fool any longer. She certainly wasn't interested in me in a romantic or sexually or even as a friend anymore unless I was touching her and she didn't have to do anything, which never felt good. I felt like I was being prostituted without being paid. Sometimes, I would get so lonely and would be craving touch. Anything really, I would spend hours in the shower just to feel the water beat down on me, touching me. It almost gave me what I was looking for, but it was never the same.

I could tell when I had had enough because every little quirk about her that I use to love would now drive me crazy. When someone's chewing starts to put you on edge the relationship clearly has major issues.

One night we were watching some teen romantic comedy. I don't even remember the title. I tuned the whole thing out. It struck me just then I had to leave her. She was healthy now and I couldn't take the abuse anymore. Being controlled all the time is overwhelming. When the credits started rolling I told her we needed to talk. I had no hesitation. I had made up my mind. We walked back upstairs towards her room and she laid their naked on her bed. You know, the come hither position. True manipulation. And for the first time I was not turned on. I wanted out. I asked her to put on some clothes because I couldn't say what I wanted with her naked. She put on a sheer nightgown still trying to manipulate the situation the best she could. Couldn't she have listened to my request just once? I couldn't take this anymore. So out it came.

"I wish I could have quit you earlier. I hope I never miss you. Even though I have been obsessed with the thought of you, my pain has just grown and grown. How could you do this to me? The future we both drew, and all the shit we've been through. Look at the life I have made for you. It was never enough and the world is what I gave to you. I use to be love struck and now I am just fucked up. I wish I had never become so close to you. It wouldn't be so hard to say goodbye."

So I told her that I would be moving out tomorrow. I had no idea where to go, but I was going.

And all she said was, "Okay. I don't need you anyway." Her words really just summed up the true situation. She had only been keeping me around because she needed me to care for her. She didn't have anyone else that would do everything and anything for her, and put up with her crap at the same time. It wasn't about wanting me or loving me. I don't know. Maybe it never had been.

I packed up my whole life into my car and carefully cleaned out my room. Other than a quick thank you note to her parents there was no trace of me left. I didn't want any loose ends. We had broken up so many times before. I wanted this time to be the last time.

I slept for a few days in the Wal-Mart parking lot in my car. I couldn't face anyone. I felt embarrassed and empty. The only place I felt safe was the parking lot because they are open twenty-four hours a day and it is well lit. I could have stayed in a motel but I had so little money I didn't want to waste it on that. I am only five foot three inches so there was plenty of space in my seat of my car. The true problem was that it was just me in there with nothing else. I was facing my emotions and thoughts straight on. Believe me it was not a time when the voices were being kind because I was having a hard day. They don't believe in kindness. I felt like I was living my nightmare.

Finally, I knew I had to tell my grandfather everything. I showed up at his house looking like crap with everything I owned in my car. The second I saw him I started crying, "Everything has fallen apart and I don't have anyone or anywhere to go." He brushed my hair out of my eyes and got me a cool face cloth. He said there wasn't anything that we couldn't get through together and he was happy I was coming to him with the truth. And then he invited me out to Friendly's for dinner and ice cream so we could talk everything through.

He was actually happy to have the truth and have me back. I explained that all this time Eva was more than my friend but my girlfriend and all the difficulties that came with that. He said he thought he knew that already but he was glad I felt comfortable enough to tell him myself. I told him that I felt like I was being taken advantage of and used and it was time I stood up for myself. I was crying the whole time and he just held my hand tight and told me that he would always be there for me and nothing could be so bad to cry over ice cream. Then he gave me a huge hug. And then laughed and asked, "You think anyone has come out of the closet at Friendly's before?" It was everything I needed.

I moved in with my grandfather which I didn't want to be a permanent situation. I immediate started applying at every job possible. I saw Eva a couple times after that. She tried to entice me at one point by placing my hands on the small of her waist. All I felt was desperation. I pulled away. It just wasn't and would never be the same. Even before anything had happened with Jordan, I told her that I had met someone else. I knew that me moving on would be a major trigger for her. I needed her to move on so I could too. In all our years, I had never made her feel rejection.

She immediately went back to California without telling me and called me out of the blue one day. She said, "I know what you did. I know what you have been up to. Good bye Sara."

And that was it. Abruptly, Eva and I stopped talking. I honestly have no idea what she was talking about. Was it a delusion? A hallucination? A moment of amnesia when I did something wrong? Or was she just looking for an out? In this abrupt phone call I realized I had never fully explained my mental disorder to her for fear she would run away scared shitless. I had tried to tell her in the beginning but she pushed me away. I probably should have been more honest but I didn't understand it fully yet myself. It was my hidden secret and the thing she probably knew but never wanted to know. In her short phone call, she never explained to me the specifics like she thought I knew what the problem was. I really have no idea if it had anything to do with my schizoaffective disorder. To this day, I have no clue. All I knew was that she wanted me out of her life. I think that it was that simple; she wanted out. And I was going to respect that choice no matter how much it hurt. She had been my best friend for over ten years. But even though I was now alone for the first time since I was sixteen, I didn't feel lonely. I had felt lonelier when I was with her than without her. I haven't seen her since. I hope she has found someone important in her life. I really want her to be happy. She deserves that much. I won't ever look her up.I have no wish to invade her life.

All this applying and job interviews were occurring at a very fast pace. I had this beautiful resume, but the response I kept getting was that I was too qualified. Too qualified is nice for you aren't good enough. On paper I was an impeccable candidate for most jobs I wanted, but the interview seemed to go sour every time. I am awkward. It is that simple. Human resources would pick up on a weird vibe and then send out their favorite, a standard form letter. I was really struggling. My thoughts seemed so unorganized. I would try and think of one thing and something totally unrelated would pop up in my head. I didn't know what to do, but what I did know is that I couldn't talk about my problem with anyone.

If someone has a physical pain, like a sprained ankle, they wouldn't be nervous or ashamed for having the problem. In fact, the pain would probably be a topic of every day conversation. No one would talk about your ailment in a hushed voice or tell you that they don't want to talk about it. But when there is a mental problem, instinctually you feel like you need to hide it. You don't want to discuss it because you know no one wants to hear it. Somehow there is a sense of fear about the whole subject of mental illness. Even the most popular of disorders are so unknown and confusing to most, which leads to putting shame and guilt on those with the disability. Because my disabilities are not immediately visible, people I don't even know ask why I am on disability. "I have schizoaffective disorder" is never my answer. I will go into all the depths of my intracranial pressure problem, but not once will I explain the important other half of me.

I kept seeing this young girl in a yellow dress with a baby blue ribbon in her hair swinging back and forth on the swing set in the front yard. She reminded me of Alice in Wonderland. She was hard to ignore since it felt like she was staring at me so hard she was looking right through my head. I would try and show her to people but they didn't see her. They would joke about the depths of my imagination. But no, she was there. She sang the "Lollipop" song over and over. I never could get her to tell me what she wanted. She would just walk off into the forest.

Within three weeks, I got a job helping an adult individual with autism, profound mental retardation, and various behavioral problems, which made the job extremely dangerous. I agreed to shitty hours and pay because I was feeling desperate. I wanted to be more independent. I didn't want to be piggybacking on my grandfather for too long. I knew he would do anything for me, but I knew the sooner I got back on my own feet the happier he would be.

The client was a thirty-year-old man living as a ten month old. He was completely unable to care for himself and incredibly dangerous. His psychiatrist had him on a very high dose of Thorazine, which made him very uncomfortable. He was unable to verbally communicate this so he would hit, kick, bite, throw his shit and run in the street naked. He always had two staff with him at all times. You worked together as a team not for household tasks, but mostly for safety. I got picked to work with a Bulgarian man named Jordan. Originally my ignorant boss with fantastic geography skills told me he was from Haiti. At the time, I was not looking for a relationship at all. I wanted to be single for a while. Plus, in the beginning I didn't necessarily see him as a love interest because I had been with girls all my life. Although he was older than me I felt like we connected on so many levels immediately. We had all of our fourteen-hour shifts together. He was the only person I worked with. We would, well, mostly he would talk the whole time and quickly we became friends.

He would talk about fleeing Bulgaria. During the communist times he was literally trapped in his own country. All the borders were sealed. Which for a claustrophobic person like Jordan, it was a nightmare. Citizens were not allowed in or out of the country unless you were someone very important meaning important with the communist party. He felt like he was in prison. And unfortunately, that is exactly what happened. He ended up in a prison inside of a prison. At the time he was deep in drugs. Opiates of any kind to be exact. He had a friend who was a doctor. And because the police were already on to him for the lifestyle that comes with taking drugs every day for years at one point he was arrested.

The cops wanted to know all about this particular doctor that was a friend of his. They told him that if he told them everything about the doctor that he wouldn't have to serve any time. So he said sure and they let him go. But that wasn't his intention. He went straight to the doctor and let him know that they were looking into him and to get his affairs in order. The police realized Jordan wasn't going to be an informant and he served one and a half years in prison at age nineteen just because he didn't want to rat out his friend and have him lose his medical license. A selfless act that I doubt many people would do. Soon after Jordan and his brother George escaped across the border into Yugoslavia with guns shooting at them all the way through.

Eventually, they made it to Italy and were homeless off and on for two years. Even though he was not a believer, George went to school and became a Priest. This allowed them a free place to live and food. Jordan ended up getting a job in construction. Or rather, digging out basements. He was also working for a moving company. At that time, Italian employers never paid on time. Maybe once a month if you were lucky. You had to constantly ask for your paycheck. They were still learning the language and had very little security. It was hard enough just to find enough food for one small meal a day. Soon they were able to move to the United States as political refugees and ended up in Maine.

We couldn't have enough of each other form the very start. We were like magnets. Immediately, we were together all the time. Inside work, outside of work, it didn't really matter where we were. But we had yet to take it beyond friendship. I remember one day after our client had gone to bed we were both doing chores around the house. I was sweeping and Jordan was sitting at the dinner table filling out the daily paperwork. I remember every detail so well. He was wearing this sky blue t-shirt that said "TRACK" with white letters on it. His jeans set loose on his hips. His body was lean and in shape from yoga. When I went by him I lightly moved my arm across his shoulders and continued to clean. I wanted him to know I was interested. He was probably confused since I had told every one at work that I was a lesbian. I had never had these feelings for any man before or since. To be honest, at that time I never really understood my emotions, my sexual identity was shifting and I didn't know how I would handle that. But deep down I knew I couldn't help myself. I think my soul knew something that my body and mind didn't know yet.

When we were all done working, the client was asleep and

we were just waiting for the time to pass as we sat on the old ratty

couch they had put in this poor guys home. We talked and moved

closer. I was so focused on my next move that I wasn't paying too

much to the conversation. After all trying to be smooth takes

concentration. He would move one inch closer and then so would I. I

would touch his knee and then he would touch mine. I could feel his

breath on my lips. My body breathed with anticipation. My mouth

was slightly dry from nervousness. I moved in for the kiss, waited,

and he came towards me. And then I kissed him. It felt perfect. I had

finally dared to take the fork in the road. The only weird thing was

that I had never kissed a guy with facial hair before. It felt very

different, not bad, just new. My heart was racing. My instincts were

taking over. I heard the next staff arriving for their shift. I tried to fix

my hair and tuck in my shirt. My face was flushed but it was too late

to change that.

When the next shift of workers came we quickly hurried out

to our cars but remained just standing there in the street staring at

each other. Under the street lamp his green eyes glowed. I was

hoping he wouldn't say goodbye. Since neither one of us wanted to

separate so Jordan invited me back to his place. I was happy and a

little nervous at the same time. I got in my car and followed him. My mind was racing so much there was no need for the radio. I loved it. I knew that our hands were meant to hold each other. Fearlessly and forever which is why it never felt like I was getting to know him. It always felt like I was remembering him from some place in my past. As if in every lifetime that we have lived we have chosen to come back and find each other to fall in love again. Over and over for all eternity. I didn't want to separate. And I just feel lucky that I found him so soon in this lifetime because all I have ever wanted to do is spend my life loving him. I was already in love. I just couldn't say it yet.

I had very little sexual experience with men before. I had been clear with him from the beginning about mostly being with women. I even had told him I didn't think it was possible for me to be physically attracted to a man. I didn't want him to find this out later and think I was making a fool of him. We went to his room and I sat on the edge of his bed nervously. I was trying to decide exactly what I wanted to happen. But I was over thinking the whole situation. I just needed to let it happen. He wasn't pushy about it at all but I knew what he wanted. I was surprised when he just took of his clothes immediately after lighting a candle. Was I ready for this?

Because of our attraction for each other we moved too quick

and too far the first night. He couldn't keep an erection and I wasn't sure I was ready for sex, which I am sure he felt. Even though I loved being so close to him, he saw it as a minor disaster. The next day I found out he was embarrassed at his performance. He said this was the first time this had ever happened to him before. This made me worry a little that I was the problem. But to me, the whole thing was wonderful. Honestly, I hadn't thought much about it. In a lesbian relationship there isn't exactly an erection to make such a big deal about. It is more about the overall enjoyment, not the exact standing power of your penis. I was so excited about everything that did happen that I didn't care what hadn't. I didn't care about an erection. The next day we talked for hours lying in bed together without doing anything except holding each other. We just needed to get to know each other better. We both confessed that neither one of us had ever moved this fast before. But after hours of talking I reached over his chest and underneath the waist of his pants and there was definitely no problem any longer. From then on there were no problems. We would have sex for hours until we were exhausted and slightly sore.

Most importantly Jordan has always been there. Through the worse times and the best. I respect him so much. Everything about him. I never ever thought I could feel this way about a man. And no, I don't think I am bisexual. I think he is the one and only exception to my rule. At first I freaked out. How could this be happening? A major part of my identity was wrapped around being a lesbian and yet there I was. What would everyone else think? Would I lose friends? More importantly, was I sure? I didn't want to just fuck with him. I already respected him too much for that. I needed to figure out where my head stood before I could move on. Could this last or would I always wish he were a girl? But all those questions quickly dissipated away. Yes, he is much older than I am, but I never saw that as mattering. As long as we both were happy who the hell cared what everyone else thought. I love him for exactly who he is. Once I had that I never doubted the relationship again. I was attracted to him both mentally and physically from the moment I was introduced to him. Sure, I didn't tell him I had schizoaffective disorder right in the beginning but it all unfolded out through my delusions and odd behavior. I finally got back on my medicine and everything got much better. Especially because he now knows the truth and is so supportive.

Within just a couple months we got our own apartment. It has been almost nine years that we have been together. I am even happier now than I was in the very beginning. He has my back and I have is. It is exactly the way it is supposed to be. I want so desperately to be there as much for him as he is for me everyday. I am so positive that only death could be what separates us. I know that I will never leave him. There is nothing else I am looking for. I can't imagine losing him. I don't think I could go on living. He is my soul mate.

~ Thirteen ~

After just six months, I got a job working with autistic children with behavioral problems at the local mental health hospital. Ironic. If it weren't a conflict of interest, it is possible that I might have been a frequent flyer of the joint.

I did not work with the general population unless there was an emergency. On the Developmental Disabilities unit, there were twelve children between the ages of three and nineteen years old. To be on this unit, the child had to be diagnosed with Autism or another pervasive developmental disorder like Asperger's. In addition, the child was over run with behavioral problems. You are always working with one child at a time and sometimes there would be two staff for one patient depending on how dangerous he or she was. The staff all had to have at least a bachelors in Psychology or higher. We got paid double what other staff did in the rest of the hospital.

Each child had a separate behavioral plan that we were to follow. For example, you set a timer for a certain amount like one minute. And if in that minute they do no exhibit any of their targeted behavioral problems they receive some sort of reward. With the lower functioning clients the reward was always given immediately, but with some of the higher functioning kids they were sometimes able to delay the reward to receive something they determined greater later on like watching a full length movie or listen to their cd player and dance in their room. Unfortunately for most, the treat was almost always food. Every child on the unit gained about thirty pounds the first month, which I never agreed with. Why couldn't they earn playtime or even a sticker instead? It never made sense to me.

They were all aggressive. Always hitting, head butting, kicking, grabbing, or breaking this or that. Often their sexuality came out in weird ways like putting their hand down your pants. Or even drawing with their own blood from their period all over the locked seclusion room walls and licking it off.

It was difficult, especially in the beginning when being head butted was something new. Or having a ten year old slide their clammy hand down the back of your pants during homeroom. The best reaction was not to react at all but simply redirect their focus back to task, which is far easier said than done.

The first time an employee was slapped or punched was always a milestone. Being attacked, especially in your face, for the first time always triggers all kinds of emotions and even your past. Those of us that had worked there for a while knew to always give someone time to deal with their emotions after that first smack in the face. Sadly, the violence got easier with time. You just had to remember that it wasn't them hitting you it was their behavior. But when aggression was so pervasive in the environment that became harder and harder to ignore. Not an easy thing to do when someone just slapped you across the face and has no remorse. When I was working with a younger child it was easier to manage with but later on in their life they got bigger and stronger than I am. The children changed into having adult bodies who were all very dangerous and unable to care for themselves.

I got hurt many times, especially in the beginning. But I got better at it. I knew the patients better. I became safe and fast with restraints. I was able to remain very calm not matter what the situation which was a quality that led me to being called to work with a child at their toughest moment. No child ever stayed less than three months and most stayed at least a year. This is different than the rest of the hospital where people stay five to six days. We had a daily schedule that was an attempt to provide the patients with a sense of security to prevent the stress stemming from not knowing what was going to happen next.

Often, I worked with our oldest patient. He was nineteen. He had been permanently thrown out of every public school in the state. Jack was extremely strong and dangerous and always had two to three staff with him at all times. He spoke but it was very little and usually didn't make too much sense. He usually expressed himself through screaming. His anxiety was through the roof several times a day. You could never relax when you were with him even for a moment because that would be just the moment he might try and strangle you. Just during his stay with us, he had already broken seven people's noses, someone's leg, and bit a huge chunk out of someone's bicep. He was no longer a child. He had become a dangerous man.

One day, I was working with him alone just for a minute while his other staff had gone to the bathroom. I felt comfortable to be alone for just a moment since he was just sitting there watching his favorite movie, Charlie and the Chocolate Family, for the one-thousandth time. An over confident mistake. And all of sudden he flew out of his chair and charged at me. Running away wasn't an option. We were in a separate room at the end of the hall. I had to close the door so he couldn't get out. I had to block him from hurting any other clients or staff that were within our proximity. I put up my hands to show him I wouldn't hurt him, but he grabbed one of them twisting it until it snapped. Finally, someone came in and helped me but it was too late. My wrist was broken in three places. I was done. I knew I would never be able to do this job again because it is so hands on.

This was a demanding job. It wasn't exactly something you could call out from last notice more than twice without them sitting you down for a chat. "We're concerned." After my injury, I wasn't able to help out with restraints any longer. I had to have microsurgery on my wrist, which led to almost a year of physical therapy to recover. Plus, now that I think of it a sense of fear had moved in which the patients could sense immediately. I was sad and I felt like I hadn't been enough, that I was a failure at the job that I once had believed I was excellent at. I had just received a promotion before I was injured to be the evening staff leader. I was pleased, but now that didn't matter. But more than that I loved my work, no matter how stressful and demanding it could be, I always came home feeling like I truly had made a difference in many individuals lives.

I went on to work for the medical records office in the administration wing of the hospital. It was less demanding and boring as hell, but I was good at it. I was twice as fast as all the other staff. It was so easy to me. I couldn't understand why the others struggled so much. I think they spent most of the day paying their bills, clipping their nails, chatting with their online boyfriend, and buying curtains for their living room on the Internet. I was always done my eight-hour shift in half the time. I would use the extra time to do homework. During the time when I was working in medical records, I received my Masters degree in Health Information Management from St. Scholastica University's online program in just one year. I was preparing myself to run the department when my boss retired which would be soon. But unfortunately, this job came to an end as well. I still couldn't do it. The headaches were drowning any success and ambition I may have had. I was vomiting during staff meetings from the pain. Sure, they said, you can work with your sunglasses on. But how many times is that really "okay" before you are a problem? I used up my paid time off and then I got approved for short-term disability. This allowed me to receive my regular pay without working for six months.

My physical and mental health was overwhelming my life. It was just one bad feeling on top of another. Often it was hard to tell what was worse the physical or the mental pain, Worst of all I felt guilty. I always feel guilty. I resigned and began the process of applying for regular disability, which they make as difficult for you as they can. Luckily, Jordan always had my back. He helped me through every step of the way. I had to make it work. I needed to be on disability. Social Security makes it so you cannot receive any income while they make there decision which takes some unknown and long period of time.

I had a long history of having the schizoaffective disorder diagnosis from multiple doctors for the past seven years and over a dozen drug trials. Luckily, my situation was made even more evident by a concise letter from my psychiatrist at the time, which basically stated in the most sophisticated language, "Sara is too crazy to work." The Social Security Administration didn't need anything else after that. It was clear I needed help. I didn't even have to get into my intense physical issues. There was no need to tell them about my increased intracranial pressure and all the lumbar punctures I had to under go to relieve the pressure in my cerebrospinal fluid. I didn't know at the time that having the diagnosis of schizophrenia is the easiest and clearest way to receive benefits. Apparently, being nuts was enough. I got approved the first time I applied only a few weeks after my interview. I was really surprised that I got approved so fast. It was such a relief. I received retroactive pay for the previous months I couldn't work within a week or so.

The worst part was that they determined that social security paid me thirty-four dollars too much to receive health insurance. I had to wait two years to receive Medicare and another three to receive long-term care Maine Care that is what I should have had from the beginning. How can you be on disability and not get health insurance? I have no fucking clue. It's cruel. I told them to take away the extra thirty-four dollars so I could get the insurance but they said

I couldn't do that.

"I can handle this." I repeat the mantra over and over, but my problems are bigger than me. And I don't want to give it to anyone else. Except I have. Before getting on the right medication, I would have to wait for hours and suffer the ugly judgment of the emergency room. Even now, I end up there several times a year. You know that they put flat screen televisions in the emergency rooms now? Yea, your own personal remote so you can catch up from missing last weeks showing of "The Bachelorette" while waiting for the nurse to finish her powdered sugar chocolate donut before she checks her e-mail. To me that is not emergency care. If I say the pain is a "ten" and then you hand me a remote control you might as well laugh in my face and stick the remote up my ass.

I have caused Jordan to suffer and worry. All things he never thought he signed up for. Phone calls. Accidents. Trips to the ATM. Not enough money. Long nights sitting in the emergency room waiting for me to get better. Sure I have prescription pain medicine but it is never enough. But he already had an addiction problem from years ago so my problems just exasperated his problem. I feel guilty about that every single day.

The best way to describe it is that your head feels like it's going to explode or implode. The pressure of the cerebrospinal fluid around my brain is too high. You have all the symptoms of having a brain tumor without having one. It was originally called Pseudo tumor Cerebri. In other words, a false brain tumor of sorts. Now it's called Increased Intracranial Hypertension (IIH). And no, it has nothing to due with high blood pressure, which is a mistake made by more idiot doctors than I can count.

But is this the worst of my problems? Or is it that my mental health is leading me to destruction? Schizoaffective Disorder is so fun to say, right? Never heard of it? Well, to put it simply, imagine Bipolar Disorder and Schizophrenia get into a car crash and fuse together in the flames. You have all the symptoms of schizophrenia along with a mood disorder which in my case is depressive.

The architecture of my mind is working against me here. No matter how many times the exterior design is changed the internal structure stays the same. And sadly it is far more stable than my pillow. The carpet provides some stabilization but what if the floor is crooked? Who planned that? Zyprexa, Abilify, Risperdal, Geodon, Haldol, Lithium, Thorazine, Cloazaril, Compazine, Seroquel. What choices. It's like the morning after Halloween – all the junk is left at the bottom of the bowl. And believe me, I have tried all of them before getting to where I am now. I am currently taking 900mg of Seroquel a night (this is considered the maximum daily dose) plus Klonopin for anxiety. It is amazing that I am not a walking zombie, but my body has slowly adjusted over time to the drugs. But that doesn't mean they still don't make me feel uncomfortable. Sometimes it still feels that way. Throughout the years of trying all the various drugs, I still have times where I am falling asleep, pacing, twitching, go weeks without smiling, and put on a good thirty pounds. It makes you feel trapped in your own skin. I wake Jordan up several times a week because of bugs on my skin or on the bed. I want to fly out of my own body, to unzip my outer coating and step out of it. This combined with the shame, stereotypes, and stigma that goes along with mental illness sometimes is too much to take.

There are still attitudes within most societies that view symptoms of psychopathology as threatening and uncomfortable, and these attitudes frequently foster stigma and discrimination towards people with mental health problems. Such reactions are common when people are brave enough to admit they have a mental health problem, and they can often lead on to various forms of exclusion or discrimination – either within social circles or within the workplace.

What is mental health stigma? Mental health stigma can be divided into two distinct types: *social stigma* is characterized by prejudicial attitudes and discriminating behavior directed towards individuals with mental health problems as a result of the psychiatric label they have been given. In contrast, *perceived stigma* or *self-stigma* is the internalizing by the mental health sufferer of their perceptions of discrimination and perceived stigma can significantly affect feelings of shame and lead to poorer treatment outcomes.

In relation to social stigma, studies have suggested that stigmatizing attitudes towards people with mental health problems are widespread and commonly held. In a survey of over 1700 adults in the UK, it was found that (1) the most commonly held belief was that people with mental health problems were dangerous – especially those with schizophrenia, alcoholism and drug dependence, (2) people believed that some mental health problems such as eating disorders and substance abuse were self inflicted, and (3) respondents believed that people with mental health problems were generally hard to talk to. People tended to hold these negative beliefs regardless of their age, regardless of what knowledge they had of mental health problems, and regardless of whether they knew someone who had a mental health problem. More recent studies of attitudes to individuals with a diagnosis of schizophrenia or major depression convey similar findings. In both cases, a significant proportion of members of the public considered that people with mental health problems such as depression or schizophrenia were unpredictable, dangerous and they would be less likely to employ someone with a mental health problem.

Who holds stigmatizing beliefs about mental health problems? Perhaps surprisingly, stigmatizing beliefs about individuals with mental health problems are held by a broad range of individuals within society, regardless of whether they know someone with a mental health problem, have a family member with a mental health problem, or have a good knowledge and experience of mental health problems. For example, it was found that stigma directed at adolescents with mental health problems came from family members, peers, and teachers. Forty-six percent of these adolescents described experiencing stigmatization by family members in the form of unwarranted assumptions (e.g. the sufferer was being manipulative) of distrust, avoidance, pity and gossip. Sixty-two percent experienced stigma from peers which often led to friendship losses and social rejection and thirty-five percent reported stigma perpetrated by teachers and school staff, who expressed fear, dislike, avoidance, and under-estimation of abilities. Mental health stigma is even widespread in the medical profession, at least in part because it is given a low priority during the training of both specialized and general physicians.

What factors cause stigma? The social stigma associated with mental health problems almost certainly has multiple causes. Throughout history people with mental health problems have been treated differently, excluded, and even brutalized. This treatment may come from the misguided views that people with mental health problems may be more violent or unpredictable than people without such problems, or somehow just "different", but none of these beliefs has any basis in fact. Similarly, early beliefs about the causes of mental health problems, such as demonic or spirit possession, were 'explanations' that would almost certainly give rise to reactions of caution, fear, and discrimination.

Even the medical model of mental health problems is itself an unwitting source of stigmatizing beliefs. First, the medical model implies that mental health problems are on a par with physical illnesses and may result from medical or physical dysfunction in some way (when many may not be simply reducible to biological or medical causes). This solely implies that people with mental health problems are in some way 'different' from 'normally' functioning individuals. Secondly, the medical model implies diagnosis, and diagnosis implies a label that is applied to a 'patient'. That label may well be associated with undesirable attributes (e.g. 'mad' people cannot function properly in society, or can sometimes be violent), and this again will perpetuate the view that people with mental health problems are different and should be treated with caution.

Why does stigma matter? Stigma embraces both prejudicial attitudes and discriminating behavior towards individuals with mental health problems, and the social effects of this include exclusion, poor social support, poorer subjective quality of life, and low self-esteem. As well as it's affect on the quality of daily living; stigma also has a detrimental affect on treatment outcomes, and so hinders efficient and effective recovery from mental health problems. In particular, self-stigma is correlated with poorer vocational outcomes (employment success) and increased social isolation. These factors alone represent significant reasons for attempting to eradicate mental health stigma and ensure that social inclusion is facilitated and recovery can be efficiently achieved.

How can we eliminate stigma? We now have a good knowledge

of what mental health stigma is and how it affects sufferers, both in terms of their role in society and their route to recovery. It is not surprising, then, that attention has most recently turned to developing ways in which stigma and discrimination can be reduced. As already described, people tend to hold these negative beliefs about mental health problems regardless of their age, regardless of what knowledge they have of mental health problems, and regardless of whether they know someone who has a mental health problem. The fact that such negative attitudes appear to be so entrenched suggests that campaigns to change these beliefs will have to be multifaceted, will have to do more than just impart knowledge about mental health problems, and will need to challenge existing negative stereotypes especially as they are portrayed in the general media.

In the UK, the *"Time to Change"* campaign is one of the biggest programs attempting to address mental health stigma and is supported by both charities and mental health service providers. This program provides blogs, videos, TV advertisements, and promotional events to help raise awareness of mental health stigma and the detrimental affect this has on mental health sufferers. However, raising awareness of mental health problems simply by providing information about these problems may not be a simple solution – especially since individuals who are most knowledgeable about mental health problems (e.g. psychiatrists, mental health nurses) regularly hold strong stigmatizing beliefs about mental health themselves. As a consequence, attention has turned towards some methods identified in the social psychology literature for improving inter-group relations and reducing prejudice. These methods aim to promote events encouraging mass participation social contact between individuals with and without mental health problems and to facilitate positive intergroup contact and disclosure of mental health problems (one example is the *"Time to Change"* *Roadshow*, which sets up events in prominent town center locations with high footfall). Analysis of these kinds of inter-group events suggests that they (1) improve attitudes towards people with mental health problems, (2) increase future willingness to disclose mental health problems, and (3) promote behaviors associated with anti-stigma engagement.

~ Fourteen ~

It has progressed so far that I couldn't bring myself to sleep tonight. My thoughts were running wild with no particular pattern. There is nothing to trigger them like wind at sea. Raging full force I cannot control them, cannot make them stop. They overcome me, torment me, and keep my weary body held captive. By the restlessness of my mind, my body, and soul cry out in vain as I lay bound in leather and chains. I am a prisoner of my own mind. How much longer must I suffer, and thus make others suffer, before I bring myself to surrender. How much longer must I struggle with this uneasiness? Not much longer. There must be a way out..

How did I get this way? Go ahead and drive yourself mad trying to blame some one or some event on the mistake that is I. After years of regret, depression, obsession I discovered that it doesn't matter. I am still a lemon. A faulty machine. Playing the blame game will get you nowhere except for further mania. It is better to just look inside and see what power you have to get yourself out of this hole.

I have tried all the antipsychotics. Attempting to find some kind of balance. The balance I was born without. After succumbing to the wrath of Seroquel for many years which has been the best of the bunch, I naively think that it is time to untie the string from my wrist and let the balloon fly off. Only one question: Will it rise high or will it pop leaving latex to fall and suffocate the yet another victim. From previous experiences I know that I must come off slowly to avoid withdrawal. Other than that I can only hope the hallucinations and delusions don't flood on like a tsunami damaging every one in its path. I can hope, but I know the truth is that all the flying daggers of this disease will all come flying back to me at once.

So why would I come off my meds? Why do I want it to stop? Why would you? I am so conflicted. I can only hope I can do this successfully on my own this time.

But every diseased person says that –

"I will be the first to cure this on my own. I don't need any help".

Yes, I admit, this isn't the first time I have stopped. I have tried to stop six previous times on my own. All resulting in relapse, losing friends, losing ambition, or losing independence to just be back on the medication again but at a higher dose this time. Or maybe the doctor adds another antipsychotic to my evening cocktail? Lovely. Deep down I know that stopping isn't the answer. So why do I put myself through this flux in the tides. It is easy to explain.

How would you like to wake up one morning unable to feel any emotion. Happiness, pain, sadness, passion, guilt, desire, success, and freedom are all dulled. And it's not a fun drug. They call it a tranquilizer but there is nothing calming about it. No high or evenness comes with it instead comes agitation, the inability to stay still, a new tick, worry, and the guilty reality that someone will have to care for me yet again. Pacing the house becomes a compulsion, but leaving the house becomes a panic attack. You feel like you are not worth anything. That any creativity, innovation, special, or distinctive quality about yourself is now gone because I am just a robot that is dull to all senses. They doctors have tried their best to make me into a walking zombie so I feel nothing bad and nothing good.

The main reason I want to have more control over my illness is because I want to have a relationship with my boyfriend, and others without them having to suffer as well. I have to put a mask on my illness. When I look in the mirror I can't see the mask but I hope other people can. I wonder what it looks like. I hardly even paint anymore. Plus, this group of meds alters your metabolism drastically making it almost impossible to not gain weight. What guy wants their girlfriend to blow up like a balloon? I know I hardly smile anymore. I try though; I really do, even if it doesn't seem like it but no one wants to live with a depressive person.

Just the other day, I was reading about how Seroquel is very desirable in prisons lately. The inmates must be so desperate not to feel that they will take anything. They must claim they have insomnia and get this shit. I can't think of any other reason people would choose to take this medication. Just as I begin to think I can be free of my medications, a depression comes over me and makes me realize how much I need those mind altering pills. Plus, even though I technically take my meds voluntarily, it seems like I have no other choice. I am literally forced to take the pills if I want to function somewhat normally and have healthy relationships despite all the dangerous side effects. There is no relief of being cured or being asystomatic. The pills help me and then they don't in so many ways.

My psychiatrist is always worried and concerned why the meds aren't stopping my symptoms. She always says that my body is just resistance to pharmaceutical therapy. So I now take Ambien so I can at least get somewhat of a decent nights sleep, but I wake up after four to five hours when it begins to wear off. Until the scientific researchers some up with something new. Here I am. Stuck. The doctor keeps trying to add another antipsychotic to the one I am already on in hopes to kill off the voices and visions. I've tried but I just can't do it. The increase dosage makes all my side effects worse. I can't sleep, I can't sit still, I gain weight and I feel like all my emotions are completely flat. I pace lap after lap around my house which drives me and Jordan crazy just in itself. Simply, it doesn't make me feel safe. So every time she prescribes another one I try it once and then stop, wait until my next appointment and see where she wants to go from here. I have so many antipsychotic drugs that I have never taken stocked up in my bureau next to my bed. I wish I could find someone that needs them so I could give them away for free to someone who needs them.

But I keep trying to make my decision going back and forth again and again. No one wants to be a burden to her partner, her best friend, and to even herself. So a full dose of antipsychotics it is then.

Separately, on top of this, the headaches are worse. Pain comes on so strong that I shudder rising quickly to a sitting position and run to the bathroom to vomit. If pain medicine is not for me than whom was it made for? For about seven years, I went through about thirty-five doctors, thirty plus trips to the emergency room before I got referred to my current neurologist. She discovered I wasn't having normal headaches, or even migraines, but that I had too much too much pressure in the spinal fluid that surrounds my brain. There literally isn't enough room for my brain so it gets pushed in from all directions from the pressure. This disorder causes you to have all the symptoms of having a brain tumor without actually having one. Luckily, she has been able to help me, but definitely not enough. My last headache lasted five days, involved two emergency room visits, and I had so much cerebrospinal fluid built up it was actually coming out my nose. I lost my vision for several hours.

I feel as though the headache in my mind is wrapped up into a ball and every once in a while it bursts open, taking over, making it impossible to think of anything else or even breathe. The voices sound just like if you were talking to me. And I can't make it stop. So much for relieving my headache. The pain worsens. It feels like my head is going to explode from too much fluid surrounding my brain. It gets worse and worse surrounding my entire brain and mind until I can't even think enough to make the next step to help myself. Would I even make it to the Emergency Room? Because of all the tests and hospital visits my veins are so hard to find it usually takes at least three nurses and six or more tries. I don't mind the needles when I am in so much pain but the delay only worsens my pain. And then the nausea and vomiting start. I have tried almost every antiemetic known. Even Marijuana makes me throw up with in seconds of inhaling. Vomiting comes on so fast and explosive I can barely make it to the bathroom. My body convulses throwing my stomach against the edge of the toilet with each spasm leaving bruises that will last over a week.

But it's one thing or the other. Headaches or bugs. Bugs? Yes.

They wake me up because they are crawling all over my legs up to my knees. I run to the shower to rinse them down the drain. I walk back to the bed to change the sheets, but no bugs. Where did they go? I search underneath the bed, in my pillowcase, and force Jordan to get out of the bed so I can look as carefully as possible. But my mind is twisted.

The mechanism of paranoia is an electrical impulse. The feeling is generated in the amygdale – of fear, of uncertainty, which the brain instantaneously turns into a "story" to make sense of it: the paranoid delusion.

What would you think if I told you that I could make the sun disappear? Would you think that I was joking? What if I believed what I was telling you without a single doubt? Would you want to believe it or even try to make it true so I would not have to face the impossibility of my statement? Or maybe you would just indulge me and ask. How? Show me. It would most certainly cause a manic response flow out of my mouth involving inventions, the Internet, aliens, celebrities and most surely every other carefully calculated idea of mine from the last two weeks. But the catch is at the time I have no idea that any of this is happening or how bizarre I must look. It is just my reality. Perhaps, because you love me, you try to imagine that I am just making a joke and sit and lightly laugh nervously. But perhaps, this has happened before one too many times and you close your eyes as your body shudders. Oh, no, not this. Not now. Not again.

The inevitable progression of my illnesses make it impossible to disappear quickly like a hailstorm. Rather it slowly came over me like walking into the ocean. Each wave washing over me bringing me just a little deeper then easing me back closer to shore giving a false sense security that I might be able to swim back to land but with each wave and strong fatigue I am officially drowning and there is no turning back.

During the day, lady number one has been in the abandoned house on the corner where I walk Liam during the week. She did come to turn on the lights yesterday. Tonight she is in there for sure. But has no lights on. It was Halloween. But she didn't give out any candy or even answer her door. Children were walking away from her house with empty bags. I know she just came to make me nervous. Flicking her lights off every seven seconds when I walked by. Plus, man number three from down the street only comes with his black truck to check his mail, yell at his pack of goats, and then leaves. His mail got delivered to my mailbox about two weeks ago.

Coincidence? Doubtful. I bet he put it there just to mess with me. Bravely, I brought it over to be put through his mail slot. No one appeared to be home. Perfect timing. But a hand appeared. He grabbed mine forcefully and let go. No words were exchange. And then black out. The next thing I remember is being on the decrepit stairs that leads an old office building. What appointment was I there for. I do not know. I had a card in my hand it said 279121628. Where was I? And then I felt it. The bump on the back of my head. The implant. The source of my disintegration. There is a secret message in the communication here or a secret plan or pattern. It must be figured out before they destroy me.

Another man, is standing at the edge of my driveway standing still. It is the dead of winter and he is just standing their completely still. How did he find me here? How could this make sense? I see him when I am grocery shopping sometimes. It makes me nervous and rude. I panic. I need to get done shopping as quickly as possible. But how did he find me here. What does he want? He hasn't tried to talk to me. He just silently stares and I can feel him watching every move. He leaves the store carrying his grocery bags back to his home, but he lives too far away to not use a car. Plus, there is no bus out this way. I am too petrified to offer him a ride.

When I get home I try to do the laundry, but all I can think is that he is watching my every move. I just want to be left alone. Why is he doing this? Now I can't leave the house or even take a shower for fear the locks won't work.

3am. The blood was streaming down the walls. This time it was Maggie doing this? She was laughing hysterically at my fear. I have sealed myself in bed paralyzed by fear. People are screaming at me when I close my eyes. I had never been so scared as I was last night. But tonight is worse. Was he trying to give me the code? He had to have been in the house somewhere. And then I saw him standing in the doorway. The light was green in the room. I lay in the bed covers on my head. Hiding until he disappeared. I didn't know what would happen.

Any friends I have ever had had even less of an understanding over what is going on with me than I do. To them it seemed like my problem is simply lying, telling fairy tales, or becoming someone new. One by one I was losing my reality, my friends, and living in an alternative universe. Now I am pretty isolated except for Jordan.

All these symptoms started a couple years before things went sour with my family so that isn't the cause of it. Two separate problems: the increased intracranial pressure causing my severe headaches and the schizoaffective disorder causing all things crazy to put it simply. They make for a fabulous combination – one increases then the other one usually does. The psychiatrist is a fabulous doctor helping me each step of the way. But my neurologist is refusing to help me any further with my pain. Isn't pain to the point of waking me up with severe vomiting the whole point of prescription pain medicine?

I am just so tired. Tired of being scared, of being in pain, of wondering if what I am seeing or hearing is real. I am tired of worrying the people in my life. And I scared I will end up like my father.

~ Fifteen ~

Attorney Parsons had her office in a somewhat renovated home in the town next to me. All of her unwise attempts at trying to settle this with my mother led nowhere. I tried to tell her that trying to just talk to her was a complete waste of time. The only thing she was able to do was to get my mother to return some of my personal items to her office. My mother left everything on her porch so I came to pick it up before it rained.

At this time, I had been barely seeing Jordan for maybe two months. I had vaguely tried to explain what the situation was between my mother and I to him. He was trying to be supportive and because he didn't have a full idea of how destructive my mother is he tried to convince me to make amends. He came with me to help pick up all my junk. About ten minutes into us moving my memories into the car my mother ran out of the bushy trees that lined the edge of the parking lot. She had been secretly watching us the whole time. Who knows how long she had been waiting there waiting to fly out of the bushes. She was now a stalker. She started crying hysterically at me. "Please talk to me. I begging you, PLEASE." I told Jordan to not say anything and get into the car with me. We drove away with her still there. I was so mortified. I was positive it would just be a matter of time before he realized he didn't want to be around such craziness. Actually, I was ready for him to blame me for her hiding in the bushes like I should hsve known she ws going to do something that crazy.. I was waiting for him to say that I should have been protecting him. But then I realized that this is what I was used to with Eva. I needed to forget about the past. He told me that he could handle the situation and that she didn't scare him. It was such a relief.

This lovely story of the destruction of my father and of my family has surely had some strange effect on me through out the years. But surprisingly, I still am able to trust. Trust for my boyfriend most of all. I am sure though that the stress of all this emotional destruction has cause so much trauma for me that at times it has inflated all of my symptoms of the schizoaffective disorder.

After this happened, I switched lawyers. I went with the original choice. Beagle was much more expensive, but he immediately won over my grandfather and I with his knowledge and confidence. It finally felt like we had a hold on the situation. But because of all my mothers continued manipulations over the following years the process went very slow. My mother tried to low ball me with offensive figures of how much she would pay me for signing everything over to her. The only way to get what she took from me was to take her to probate court. Maybe this sounds simple, but it took several years before the day of our trial.

I was so nervous my asthma raised its nasty head while I was waiting to walk into the courtroom. I was sweating profusely. I had spent so much energy making sure my mother didn't know who I had become or where I was living that letting even her be able to see me was incredibly nerve wracking. All I could think was she was going to hurt me in some way or figure out who Jordan was and get to him. I even purposely had him not come to the case so she wouldn't get any ideas of how to mess with him. I felt like something truly horrible was about too happen.

Surprisingly, when I walked into the courtroom with my lawyer a wave of calm washed over me. I realized how far I was from her now. I was so much stronger now. She almost seemed like a stranger. I knew there was nothing she could do to bring me down and this whole process would be about getting back exactly what she had taken from me. Her true persona would be exposed. Her presence no longer bothered me. I was stronger than I thought. I felt so powerful in that moment. I had finally moved on.

The three-day trial helped me to move on emotionally. My mother did not have a lawyer. She defended herself poorly. My mother lied so many times on the stand the judge almost threw her out. He fined her for contempt three times over the course of the trial. Then as she was saying her closing argument she turned to my lawyer and I and told us to stop laughing. We hadn't even made a noise. The judge told her he would not have such behavior in his courtroom. I finally found like I had been spending all this money and all these years fighting her for a reason. Everyone could see how abnormal she is. Thanks to my grandfather I had my life back. It wasn't hers anymore. I was my own person. The judge ruled in my favor.

When we were all collecting our paperwork after the trial my mother's husband snuck behind me when I wasn't paying attention. He whispered to me, "You always have a place with me no matter what happens." How creepy! His breath smelt like it had come out of his asshole. How could she even kiss him? Or did she? I had only met him twice before very briefly many years ago. He didn't know anything about me and I didn't about him. What was he even talking about? His breath smelt like a hot pile of shit. Did he live in a fantasy world just like my mother?

When grandpa found out about the ruling I finally saw some relief in his face as well. He died only a couple months later before I received any money, but at least he knew that he had helped give me security and love because everything was going to work out. Unfortunately. I didn't realize that just because the judge had ruled in my favor that in order to get the money she owed me it would be a whole other extensive process.

While trying to come sort of arrangement, my mother

decided to file for bankruptcy. It was obvious she had plenty of money, properties, and other investments. In a slimy move, she switched most everything in her husbands name and then claimed she had nothing so I couldn't get to it. The judge thought it would be easiest if we tried to solve this through mediation. I really did not want to see her again, but this time I knew that I could do it. Plus I had my main lawyer Alan Beagle plus his partner Jenn and my bankruptcy lawyer all their to support and guide me through the whole situation. I was more than strong enough this time. This time she showed up with a lawyer, but he couldn't do much. She started crying many times throughout the meeting trying to get the process to stop or to get a break. She said she was disabled and couldn't handle the mediation process. The mediator told her that any personal problems she may have were not to be part of this process. She told her that this was a business issue, not a personal one.

Even though, the verdict was completely in my favor, I wouldn't be able to do anything until the court could figure out a way to get the money from her. I knew she would stretch this all the best she could. We finally came to an agreement. The rest of the land, twenty-eight acres, which surrounded my former home, would go up for sale immediately. We would each get our halves from the sale but then in addition she owed me in my part from her selling house illegally. The rest of the money would come in payments over the next several years and at the end of that I would receive the final chunk. Right now I am two years into the yearly payments.

I was afraid it would take forever to sell the land. The economy was in a hole and it seemed like everything else had taken an eternity, but I lucked out. The land was purchased within a month of putting it up for sale. At that point Jordan and I were struggling financially because he lost hours at work, I was on disability, and I was trying to pay my lawyers. The rent was killing us. We almost always paid late.

I started to look for house to buy. In my mind, it was the only thing this money was for. It was what my grandpa and I had been trying for all this time. And Jordan agreed it was the best and only choice for our money to go toward. All I really wanted was a place I could call home.

I started to scour the Internet for the perfect place. We wanted to move out of the city and have more privacy. Jordan wanted a house on the water but it was hard to find one in our price range that didn't need serious renovations. We both agreed that we would choose a home that we didn't have to buy a mortgage with. Most places had a small lot and we didn't want to see someone else out of every window. I came across a place near Sebago Lake that was under foreclosure. There was nothing wrong with it. It was in move on condition. We both liked it immediately. Once the bank agreed on our bid we moved into what is now our home just before the closing.

Just as the court case with my mother was starting to come to a close my grandpa's lung cancer had reached its final stage. He had already been through several surgeries and rounds of chemotherapy with radiation. I was surprised that he fought against it for so long. He got pneumonia one final time and ended up in the hospital. One day I came in while he was sleeping. I sat their silent holding his hand listening to the soft whistle in each breath he took. Suddenly, a tear rolled down my cheek. Until then I hadn't realized how sad I was. He was and had always been the most constant and important person in my life. He opened his eyes and tightened his grip.

"Sara, it's time." He swallowed hard. "I'm ready."

I knew exactly what he meant. I held my breath until I couldn't. Deep down I knew he was right. It was a decision that wouldn't be taken back. I didn't want him to suffer anymore. He had done everything he had wanted to in his life. This felt natural, not traumatic. We sat in silence together until the sun set.

The very next day I went and made all the arrangements so he could go home right away. I knew he wanted to be home. At this point there was no reason for him to be stuck in the hospital. I got all the necessary medications to make him as comfortable as possible. The next morning I brought him home. I had a bed set up in the middle of the living room so there would be enough room for any visitors he wanted. I dressed him up in his favorite tan outfit and tucked him into bed.

"Thank you for everything you have done for me. I am so lucky to have you in my life. You will be in my heart forever. I love you." He told me he loved me. I kissed him on the forehead and prepared him a syringe of liquid morphine. I held it up to the light and it twinkled blue just like his eyes. I did this many times over the course of the day. Slowly he breathing became more shallow and relaxed at the same time. Even though he was breathing, I could feel he was already gone.

He died very early that next morning. My head was lying on his chest when he took his last breath. My sadness came later. At that moment I felt a surprising feeling. Happiness. Love is watching someone die.

~ Sixteen ~

Before we moved into the house we have now, we were living in a tiny apartment in Portland on a very busy street with rent that was way too high. Where we were living before was nicer, but we weren't allowed any pets. Mostly, we moved because I desperately wanted a dog. I can't have children and my motherly instincts, I suppose, were starting to kick in. After a ton of research, I realized that a Chihuahua would be perfect for me. They are incredibly smart and personable. Since I am not the most active person I didn't want a dog that had to do a ton of running every day, but rather short walks throughout the day. If they are pure bred, which is what I wanted, they are the healthiest of dogs. They live the longest of any breed. And of course they are simply adorable. I wanted a dog I could connect with on a deep level.

Over the Internet, I found a local Chihuahua breeder who has a positive reputation lasting decades. I must have looked at the three available brother puppies online every fifteen minutes until finally they reached 8 weeks old and could leave their mother. At last, my boyfriend and I drove to the breeder. I couldn't wait to meet the beautiful Chihuahua puppies so we could see their personalities. The moment I went into her living room I saw this small quiet puppy sitting alone on the couch. The rest of the Chihuahuas were running all around playing. I sat with him and immediately fell in love. This was the one. I knew it. I would call him Liam.

While sitting beside him for the first time, I began to open up to the breeder who told me she had breeding and training Chihuahuas for 33 years. She was very easy to talk to so I told her about my journey with mental illness. She asked me what I was still struggling with in my life. I told her I was annoying my boyfriend. She laughed. I explained that I ask him constantly, "Did you hear that?" or "Did you see that?" to reality check the low level hallucinations that my medicine doesn't completely take care of. As you can expect, this was creating a very stressful household. Jordan was burned out. We needed a change. I was also scared to be home alone and to go out alone mostly because of paranoia and being self conscious of my possible behaviors. She said she had some ideas on how Liam could help me, but she had never tried them before. I immediately thought of hugs, kisses, and unconditional love, which are all wonderful but I didn't know how else she could train Liam to help me. I told her I couldn't pay and she said all she wanted was to be part of something that could be miraculous. How could I resist? I was so curious about her ideas that I agreed to work with her to train him to be my service dog. I worked with her for two years, and for the second year my therapist even agreed to join us. This was the opportunity of a lifetime. I'm so thankful.

After a lot of work on all from all of us (Liam most of all), Liam now assists me in ways I never thought possible. The most supportive and unique way he helps me has been life changing. With Liam, when I lightly tap his shoulder with two fingers and then ask him either "Did you hear that?" or "Did you see that?" if he did he will put one paw forward and if he did not he will lay down. Super amazing, right? This seemingly basic task continues to change the way I live my life every day. I don't have to ask the people closest to me a thousand times a day about what I am seeing or hearing. My paranoia has decreased drastically. I'm not scared to be home alone and I'm not scared to go out alone because he is always there supporting me.

He came home wrapped in a flannel green blanket. He only weighed two pounds with distinct black and white features. Quickly, he has grown to a full six and a half pounds with a charming personality. If he isn't happy, I am not happy and visa versa. He is incredibly loving, healthy, and a great companion. He comes with me wherever I go; public speaking engagements, errands, planes, hospital visits, museums, everywhere. He is most certainly a part of the family. Not just for me, but for Jordan as well. I like to think that we have an invisible leash connection at all times.

Moving into your first home is very exciting. I was so ready for the responsibility. This past year has been spent slowly making this our place in every way. The house was in move in condition when we bought it, but only now does it completely feel like home. I finally have painted the walls, hung up all our favorites, and tweaked the rest. I almost feel totally relaxed. There are no arguing couples upstairs or rent that we need to pay. We have plenty of land and our only neighbors are hardly ever home. It helps me to remain in a calmer state because I don't start worrying what I heard upstairs or across the street. For the must part, it is very quiet here. Since the house was under foreclosure we got about one-third off the regular price.

Despite this beneficial home life I have, lately I seem to be undergoing a relapse of my own kind. Switching medication in an effort to control a side effect from antipsychotics now has caused me to be depressed. I see my psychiatrist pretty much every six weeks or so. At this point, we both know that the medication is absolutely essential to control my symptoms, but at the same time the dangers of the antipsychotics are so severe at times she is in limbo. I have developed a somewhat severe swallowing problem due to the medication. The voices in my head are louder than they have been in a while. I tried talking to Jordan about what was going on with me, but he said, "That's too much to talk about right now. I try to think of good things." I can understand this and I really don't want to stress him out, but sometimes I feel so alone and not alone at the same time. I feel like I can never be truly alone because of the circus in my head.

What caused this relapse? Maybe it is because my increased intracranial pressure has been worse lately or maybe is it just some kind of genetic imbalance of my brain that just happened to increase right now. I try to smile, be pleasant, but I am aware that I just come across as depressed or distant.

Larry and Maggie, the fantastic pair that have taken up residence in my mind for many years now have come back. They are unrelenting and are against most everything I do. They are a pair, a force, making them much more believable then just one voice. Imagine you're at a party and you end up next to the couple that is constantly arguing. That is what it is like to have them in my head.

Before I close my eyes at night I think about the day and the universe and all the things I have to be grateful for and I try to not think of Larry and Maggie because it hurts. I am not thankful for that, for that pain. I am sure that I sleep with my mouth open because when I wake I can taste Larry in my stomach. There are small pieces of him between my teeth.

You're in my stomach and windpipe crawling in and out and squeezing and shutting down my heart. Sometimes you get stuck, preventing me from being able to swallow. I gag on my own nightmare. Making it difficult for me to get the words out and the newness in. You are a familiar taste, but that doesn't mean I like your bitterness. Imagine uncooked rhubarb, stout beer, and some unsweetened coffee. All topped of with the dandelion greens you tried when you were four. You seep through my tongue, spreading out and sitting stubbornly on each taste bud. You stain my lips.

When I shower in the morning, I brush my teeth three times. I spit you out and brush again and again. Just to be sure I open my mouth to let the jets of water spray into my mouth, onto my gums, on each side of my tongue trying to get rid of you for at least a moment. But it's too late. You crawled inside of me at night through the doorway of dreams. You flood on in but do not know the way out. My mind is like a lobster trap. Everything in and nothing comes out. I run my tongue along my teeth. It feels so unfinished. Flickering remains. I flossed last night but yet this morning there you were – another thought – another piece of you.

How am I supposed to forget, promise myself to move on, to stop the obsession?

Brush. Spit. Rinse again. And again.

You give me heartburn.

Freeze the moment. Please, all I'm saying is wait, just wait, just, just...please hear me out because this is more than I can take. Call it whatever you want. An episode, a relapse, madness, or just plain crazy, get me out of here. Now. Right now. I'm begging you. Oh, am I bothering you...Is this too uncomfortable? You can't stand it, but you tell me "it's okay to be uncomfortable. Just embrace it!" I have heard it all. "You know some people don't do anything for their pain." Or my favorite, "We don't need to talk about this. I don't want you to get all upset." Which really means, please stop. You're making me so uncomfortable! People say, "Best if we don't consider how you got here." Or "You may have to live with it, but I don't." And then, their eyebrows rise along with their voice because they have a "GREAT" idea -- "Have you tried earplugs?" How do I even answer such a stupid question? You look out from those eyes. Pretending to be mine, pretending to care, to be there. But you're not. You can't. It's too dark in here for you. The filaments are broken. No matter what time of day. Conversing day after day with myself, my separate realities. I am being swallowed by my own oxygen. I am sure earplugs will help with that. Can you jam them in tighter for me? "That's helping right?" Said with an exaggerated smile and strained thumbs up. I give one right back. "Yeah, the earplugs are working

GREAT. "

Did that sound too bitter? Well, at least it's an honest emotion.

So what helps me when things get worse? When I have a bad day that causes me to see 50 spiders on the wall in the middle of the night what can I do to help myself and how could someone help me? There are 3 ways. The first is asking Liam. The second is having a camera with me. If I take a picture of the hallucination or a video and then look at it only 10 seconds later the hallucination does not translate to the picture. When I first tried this I would doubt my camera, but now with increased insight about my illness and having done it so much it is now a simple and quick way to help me to move on. The third option is to ask myself or have someone ask me reality based questions without being condescending or judgmental in any way. For example, how do you think all those spiders got on the wall that quickly? What kind of problem do you think we have in the house? Were there spiders on the wall before you went to the bathroom? Slowly with more and more questions, pretty soon I will look over at the wall and there won't be any spiders there anymore. The questions will have broken down the hallucination and brought me back to reality.

I am hopeful that things will get better again with time. I just have to try and not let myself get sucked in too deep so I can still pull myself out. Finally, the rest of my life is coming together in a way I never thought possible and most people never get to experience. I have a beautiful new house and get to share it with a man for who I have all consuming love. And for the most part I think he feels the same.

All I can say is that I try. I try everyday to work on my recovery. And you know what? Trying is enough. I am motivated to learn something new about my mental health every day. Recovery for me is not about one single thing that changed my life, but rather like an imaginary tool box. In the tool box, I continue to fill it up with all my education, resources, treatment teams, and coping skills. When I ever feel like my symptoms are getting worse I know how to advocate for myself, who to call, how to ask for help, and how to help myself. So I am not scared anymore that I will end up how I was back in college because I am ready. Recovery is a process and I am always working on it.

I can't be scared because when fear is gone life opens up all of its grandeur. I have to be tough. I can't let this beat me. Strength is nothing about external performance. It is about internal belief. I realize now I am a survivor. I am a stronger woman for opening my eyes and stepping away from someone who didn't respect herself and would never respect me.

Without suffering I would never be able to savor all that I reach out to and all that comes to me like something as little as a kiss from my puppy.

UPDATE

3 years later in Spring of 2017

The last three years have been life changing in so many positive ways. I was very nervous to publish this book and have all the intimate details of my life out there in the world. I didn't know how people would react, but overall I have received so much support. Shortly after publishing this memoir I brought it to Portland, Maine's Annual NAMI (National Alliance on Mental Illness) walk and festival. I was able to share my story with so many that were feeling alone which was all I had ever hoped for when writing this book. I was very fortune to be sitting beside a woman named Nancy who happened to be selling her novel as well. She told me about a speakers bureau called Voices of Recovery that was looking for new voices to share their personal lived experiences with mental illness. I was immediately interested and have now been speaking for Voices of Recovery for three years. I am on the steering committee and I am the facilitator for their online presence. Currently, I also speak for NAMI's and Shalom House's speakers bureaus as well.

I share my journey with professionals going into the field,

college and high school students, peer groups, family members, police officers and many other audiences throughout Maine. Speaking continues to give me a sense of purpose and pride, which is so important because without pride we lose hope. Sharing my story has given me so much confidence. I no longer feel like I need to omit details about my life when speaking with anyone or feel as though I should whisper about my illness. I am now proud to say yes, I have schizoaffective disorder and look what I have done with my life.

My partner and I just celebrated twelve years together. I have so much to thank him for because I know many people would not have been able to understand or handle all that comes with my illness. So many people talk about finding true love and I feel so lucky that I found it.

I am on the verge of publishing my second book which is fiction this time around. The Audacity of Robyn is about an only child from an upper class family in the countryside of upstate New York during the beginning of the 1900's. Robyn Caldwell struggles with both her gender identity and sexual orientation from an early age. Through her journey to find her true sense of self she faces significant social anxiety, loneliness, and depression. Eventually through many courageous endeavors, Robyn discovers true happiness, confidence, and respect for herself in ways she never thought possible.

I continue to bring Liam, my Chihuahua, everywhere I go. He is still happy and healthy. The little guy just turned 7 years old last week so we are in a fantastic rhythm together. As I mentioned before, I had gotten to the point where I was scared to be alone, scared to go out alone, and causing a lot of stress in my relationships, especially with those I am closest to. While my medication (which I have been taking as prescribed) controls my delusions completely, I am left with low level hallucinations. For example, may see bugs in the bed or hear whispering that is not real. Now I can ask Liam. His little 6 pound frame has changed my life. I am not scared anymore and my relationships are stronger and healthier than ever before. He has helped me so much to reintegrate back into society.

Our lived experience – our stories - is where the power and impact lies to change lives, create system change and help eliminate the stigma surrounding mental illness and suicide. The sharing of our personal stories helps to increase understanding and awareness of risk factors and warning signs for mental illness and suicide, educate the public about mental health, mental illness, and recovery. I want to continue to be part of the movement to stop stigma against mental illness, reach as many different groups in the community as possible, and most of all to help others know that they are not alone. Mental health does not discriminate. We are all connected. We are all affected.

THE END